WRITING TO PUBLISH
A Roadmap to Success

Rebecca Waters

Writing to Publish: A Roadmap to Success
© **2021 by Rebecca Waters**
All rights reserved

Release Date: March, 2021

ISBN: 978-0-578-88306-9

No part of this publication may be reproduced, distributed, or transmitted in any form or by any means, including photocopying, recording or other electronic or mechanical methods, without the prior written permission of the publisher, except in the case of brief quotations embodied in critical reviews and certain other noncommercial uses permitted by copyright law. For permission requests, contact the publisher using the information below.

Short Iron Press
5771 Zaring Drive
West Chester, OH 45069

Table of Contents

Welcome

Part I: Developing Habits Leading to Success as an Author

Part II: Designing a Business Plan for Your Writing

Part III: Marketing You and Your Writing

Resources

About the Author

Welcome to Writing to Publish. You picked up this book because you are a writer and you want to be an author. The difference? A writer writes. An author publishes.

To have a successful writing and publishing career you need more than a computer, a dictionary, and an idea…

Think of your writing as your career. It may be a part-time job for you in the early stages, but viewing your craft as work will help you understand the elements described here as your work duties or job description. This book is a compilation of three short handbooks on writing, first published as e-books in 2017. Additional material and updates make this a readable and *reasonable* tool for any writer with the desire to publish. This book is divided into three parts:

- ✓ Developing habits leading to success,
- ✓ Designing a business plan for your writing and
- ✓ A start-up plan to market you and your writing.

Each part should be helpful on its own. In other words, feel free to access the parts of the book you need immediately. Use the book as a handbook of sorts. It is a tool to remind you of your quest and a roadmap to get to your destination.

Part I: Developing Habits Leading to Success as an Author- Successful writers employ five habits on a regular basis. This section is designed to introduce you to these five practices. These habits can become part of your writing DNA, shaping your mindset as you write and setting you on the direct path to publication.

Part II: Designing a Business Plan for Your Writing- Think of a business plan as a road map to get you to your destination. This section will take you through the process. A writing plan is similar to any business plan in that you will have a mission and vision statement as well as immediate, midterm and long-term goals and objectives, and a budget.

Part III: Marketing You and Your Writing- Marketing is an essential element of any business plan and weighs heavily on the shoulders of the author. Gone are the days of publishers flying authors to events and organizing big book signings with plenty of fanfare. Authors today must accept a growing role in marketing their own books. That begins by marketing you and your work to an agent, publisher, and readers.

If you are writing as an exercise in self-therapy, you need not read beyond this point. If, however, you long to publish your work, to make a living as a freelance writer, to see your book on the library shelf, or to watch for your name in the credits at the end of a movie, then stay with me.

How to Use This Book

How you get the most out of this book depends on your specific needs. Do not think you must start at the beginning and work your way through to the end. And don't think Part III on marketing is at the end because that is when you begin to market you and your book. Marketing will be happening as your write.

I recommend reading Part I first if you are a new on the scene writer. The habits you develop early on will serve you well throughout your writing career. If you are a seasoned writer but see the need to be more intentional in pursuing publication, you may want to go directly to Part II and create a business plan for your writing.

I've left space for your write and plan and dream. I have given you assignments for each section. I recommend you complete those (and no, you will not be graded) and date them. Later, you will easily see how you are growing and changing over time.

Part I: Developing Habits Leading to Success as an Author

The e-book version of this section was called *Writing With E's*. It is a description of five habits successful authors employ on a regular basis. Developing these five habits will breathe life into your writing and sustain you through the hours of drafting, editing, and revising. These practices will become an essential part of your writing to publish mindset.

The five elements we will examine in this section all begin with the letter E, hence the name *Writing with E's*.

What do your think these terms suggest for you as a writer? Write one or two sentences for each.

Exercise

Edit

Educate

Engage

Evaluate

Exercise Your Writing Muscle

If you wish to medal as an Olympic swimmer, you need to swim. If your goal is to win a chair in a symphony orchestra as an accomplished French horn player, you must practice. Basketball players are hailed as stars of the team after countless hours working on drills.

To be a good writer, a published author, you have to write. I know. I can hear you saying, "Duh!"

The truth is that many would-be authors do not spend time practicing their craft. Perhaps it has something to do with school. Remember when your teacher put a prompt on the chalkboard on Monday and asked you to complete the writing exercise in twenty minutes? On Tuesday you revised it in the twenty-minute timeframe, on Wednesday you edited it and on Thursday you rewrote it in your best penmanship to turn in for a grade.

Friday? Well, I don't know about your teacher, but on Friday my teacher put music on and turned off half the florescent lights so we could free write. Because she never read any of the Friday papers, a few classmates spent the time writing notes to friends or decorating their notebooks with flowers and the names of the newest love interest.

It's not that the writing program was bad, but it wasn't great either. And it could be downright harsh if your teacher wrote a disparaging remark on one of your essays or made you read what you produced to the entire class as an example of *what not to do*.

We walk away from those writing activities vowing to never torture ourselves again. Yet, if we are to strengthen our skills, we need to exercise our writing muscles.

Writing to Publish: Part I

> **Just as practicing the scales and chords on your piano helps you with hand position, sound, and note reading, practicing your writing on a regular basis helps you with structure, editing, and voice.**

Writing exercises get your brain working and the creative juices flowing. A body of evidence in brain research supports the notion that engaging in the act of writing triggers the brain to create. We become more focused and remember details when we put them down on paper. This is part of the reason I advised my university students to start writing when they came to an essay question that stumped them "Start with restating the question or write down 'I'm not sure I remember much about the theories of language acquisition…but…'" When you begin to write, something fires in your brain. The more you write, the more you remember and the more you have to say on the subject.

Composing on a computer also serves to engage the mind and helps the author get the creative juices flowing. I have often had a chapter to draft or a story to complete and a blank screen in front of me. If I don't open my computer or pick up a pen and start the activity, my brain stays in its sad holding pattern. Putting something down on paper or typing anything into my computer gets my mind focused and moving in the right direction.

As a side note, I find if I am having a severe case of writer's block, the pen and paper method of starting to write moves my thinking in the right direction faster than drafting something on the computer. Both will get me there, but for me there is something about doodling my way across the paper that triggers my creative juices. Find what works best for you.

> **To get it done you have to get it started.**

Let's look at a few ways to get your work done and develop your writing muscle. Although there are limitless ways to accomplish this, I'm offering you a choice of six activities you can start using today to strengthen you writing skills. I urge you to include at least one writing exercise in your daily or weekly routine. I chose these specific exercises because the benefits include more than improving your writing. For that reason they are sustainable.

Think of them the way you approach physical exercise. Your doctor says you need to exercise to improve your cardiovascular system. He suggests you walk 10,000 steps a day. You can get on a treadmill and reach that goal or you can walk to your local store instead of getting in a car. Personally, I prefer walking that takes me somewhere. The same is true of the six writing activities I've included in this chapter. Like any good exercise program, start with a few stretches. Get out of your comfort zone to strengthen your writing muscle.

Writing Prompts

Nearly anything can serve as a writing prompt. You can find lists of writing prompts online. You can find calendars with intriguing questions for each day or pictures to serve as a prompt. I was given a book of quotes one Christmas. Those have served as prompts from time to time.

Try this one. Write a short story about each member of your family. Call on each member's character traits. For example, include the way Uncle Joe scratches his head and looks down when he's embarrassed, or the way your sister works the name of her newest love interest into every conversation. Characterization is a powerful tool for authors.

Need to work on effective dialogue? Draft a short exchange between two members of your family.

Here's another use of those crazy characters you already know and hopefully love: describe each member of your family without using too much narrative. *Show* your reader the members of your family without *telling* the specifics. Here is a brief example:

Chris pulled the dining room chair as close as she could to the kitchen counter, stood on the seat and stretched. *Not enough.* She was about to climb onto the countertop when a long arm slipped past her and took the candy jar off the shelf.

"Here you go, Squirt." Andy tugged Chris's dark, curly ponytail.

"Thanks, Andy." Brothers could be so confusing. One minute he says she's a brat and throws a pillow at her. The next minute he helps her get into the forbidden candy jar.

Yes, it is a short example, but from it you should know a bit about Chris and Andy. You know their relationship. What can you guess about their ages? Their height? What do you know about their physical features?

Writing a short story about those crazy characters you call family could produce a new idea for a character in your latest novel. At the very least, you will preserve your family history for the best audience you'll ever know.

<u>Here's another exercise.</u> Try your hand at writing greeting card messages. I decided to write a greeting card for each member of my family. It's a great exercise because you have to communicate as much as you can in a few short sentences. This activity gets my creative juices flowing.

<u>A-Z</u>. I've also participated with others in an "alphabet" prompt where the goal is to write a blog post for every letter of the alphabet. For the blogger participating in the alphabet challenge, you will have twenty-six new and creative blog posts. If you are writing non-fiction, imagine the challenge of creating those twenty-six posts in your area of expertise.

There are benefits to using writing prompts. Writing prompts challenge you to become a stronger writer, but as you can see, prompts can also lead you to short stories, blog posts, and new characters for your book. To get you started, I've included a few prompts in the resource section of this handbook. Use them as warm-up exercises.

Queries

Journals and magazines usually require writers to pitch an idea to them first by way of a query letter. Drafting a query helps you research and outline your article, and if you are a novelist, it helps you learn the elements of a book proposal on a much smaller scale.

I like using queries as writing exercises. I think it is part of my psyche. As I said before, I'm the kind of person who isn't going on a run just for the fun of it or for exercise. I like to have a destination. The same is true in my writing. I like the carrot dangling out in front of me. I like purpose in my writing. Using query writing as a writing exercise has great benefits.

Here's how I do it. I find a publication I like and look at the types of articles they print. I grab a topic or theme suitable for the publication, research it, and develop an opening line as well as list at least three points to include in the article. I make my proposal (i.e., "a 1,500-word article looking at…") and include my bio. I put it away for a day or two before I read it out loud, edit it, reread it and send it off to the acquisitions editor for the publication. Sometimes I get the job. Sometimes I don't.

Here's why the query exercise works for me:
1. I'm writing about a topic I already find interesting.
2. I'm honing my research skills.
3. I'm outlining.
4. I'm learning ways to grab a reader with an opening line.
5. When my query is accepted, I already have completed the research and outlined the story. I write it up, get paid when it's published and add the article to my writing resume. It lets future publishers or agents know I can meet a deadline and work with an editor. I'm publishable.

Don't know where to start? First, consider the periodicals you like to read. You can check their website for submission guidelines. I use the current *Writer's Market*. You can purchase one or check one out at your library. *Writer's Market* is published annually.

The guidelines for publications rarely change significantly, but they do change. If you use an older version of *Writer's Market*, look up the publication online as well. The beauty of *Writer's Market* is that you will discover new publications you never knew existed. You will find new venues for your writing for which you are a perfect fit.

Go through *Writer's Market* and put sticky tabs on the next five markets to query. Consider each query a writing exercise.

For your convenience I've placed a very basic template for writing a query in the resource section of this handbook. It's a starting point. Be sure to follow specific directions given by the publication regarding submission.

Themed Publications

Themed publications provide great opportunities to flex your writing muscle. In this case, you write on a topic chosen by the book or magazine. Often, instead of the query, you write specifically to the topic, submit your work and pray they accept it.

When I decided to pursue a writing career, I was looking for prompts to hone my writing skills. I came across the *Chicken Soup for the Soul* website, selected four of the eight upcoming topics and drafted a story from my personal experience for each. After putting each story through a series of revisions and a significant amount of editing, I submitted three of the stories online. Two of them were accepted. It was a real boost to my writing career –an affirmation that I was on the right path. Check the *Writer's Market* or *Writer's Digest* for other possible themed publications.

Another exercise I pursued was to write an article for a home health journal. This was a themed issue on working with clients in hospice care. I've never worked in the health care industry. I was clueless about the topic and audience. However, since research is one of my strengths, I accepted the challenge.

The article was to inform home health aides about medicines their clients may be taking while in hospice care. I had to research the medicines and I had to research my audience. I used this writing assignment as an exercise in researching and writing. The article was accepted for publication, but more importantly, learning about the role of the home health aide answered a problem I had in a book I was crafting. Writing in a home health aide as a new character to engage in conversation with my main character when she came home from the hospital provided a wonderful solution to my dilemma. This is another great example showing how exercises can benefit your writing.

Contests

I interviewed with an agent at the first writing conference I attended. What I viewed as being honest came off as wimpy and unprepared. (More about that in this guide on engaging with others.) She asked if I had ever entered a writing contest. I figured my lack of confidence prompted the question. She said to come back when I had entered a few contests and had applied what I learned to my writing. Ugh!

The next agent I met was a kind man who listened carefully to my pitch.

> "I have a compelling story about a woman, a drunk driver, and family forever changed…"

> "Have you ever entered a writing contest?" he asked me, a few minutes into our time together. "As a new writer on the scene, I think you'd find it helpful."

I've heard other authors talk about this issue of "contests." The general consensus is that agents like to know you've covered the contest ground.

One highly respected literary agent shared his thoughts on contests and why some agents pose this question to writers they meet. "My take is that publishers like doing deals with the winners of writing contests. It gives them a bit of confidence that the person can write."

Participating in a writing contest helps build a writing resume. Through the contest process, writers learn how to set up submissions according to publication guidelines and meet deadlines as well. These requirements help writers develop skills needed to become published authors.

For some writers, contests are a great way to get a start in writing. Some of them have a specific question to be addressed or a topic to be explored. A few of them are genre specific (i.e., a short story romance or mystery) while others may be word count specific, as in the area of flash fiction. I recently looked into a contest where each 1,000 word (or less) short story was to be built around a life lesson learned. The theme is the prompt. The word count is an exercise in making every word of value. That makes me a stronger writer.

Although I missed the deadline on the flash fiction contest, I recast the main character's situation to create a subplot in a subsequent novel. I lifted the setting from that story and used it in a current project. My words were not wasted on my attempt for the contest.

Most contests offer you feedback. An honest critique from someone other than your mother is worth the $25 entry fee. As a side note, if you win the contest you often win a monetary prize in addition to publication.

Another "contest" you can enter is a writing challenge that takes place every November. It is called NaNoWriMo. The letters stand for National Novel Writing Month. The challenge is to draft a 50,000 word novel in one month. That shakes out to an average of 1,667 words a day if my math is right.

It is a *draft* and every word counts. Misspelled words and repetitive words you'll later erase –every word counts. There's no stopping to edit. No time to revise. Everyone who finishes the "race to write" with 50,000 words is a winner.

Can you do the same thing without signing up for the free NaNoWriMo experience? Of course, though there are significant benefits to participating.

The first benefit is that you have a powerful online support system. There are blogs and daily inspirational posts to keep you going. You will connect with other writers and cheer each other on, as well as have access to experts who will field your questions with patience. You report your word count daily. Totals are kept for you as you progress through the challenge. You are a winner in my book even if you don't reach your 50,000 word goal. If you participate, write daily, and finish the month strong, you are that many more words toward completing your manuscript. That's a contest with punch!

Blogging

When I decided to become a published author I had no idea what a blog was and no intent to write one. I had heard of them. I thought they were something akin to a public diary. A few students on the campus where I taught shared their blogs. I wasn't impressed.

At my first writing conference, I learned that other writers were maintaining blogs. During lunch, they offered advice on how to set up a blog and shared examples of how they used it. They threw words around like "platform" and "audience." I was clueless. But if I needed a blog to be a writer, I decided right then I would have one.

I spent the next five months researching blogging, signing up for free webinars on the subject, and reading the blogs of other writers. I mapped out a few posts, secured a blog name (*A Novel Creation*), and launched my blog for new writers in January of 2013. I post once a week. Every week. Consistency is crucial. With that commitment I have become stronger at writing and self-editing.

If you blog you always have something to write and a deadline to meet. You will strengthen your research skills. A bonus is found in the connections you will make with the writing community. Maintaining a blog on a consistent basis shows a future publisher your commitment to your work. It helps you with time management.

Also, I encourage writers to keep at least one potential guest post prepared and in a blog file. I have often been contacted to be a guest on a blog. Instead of being stressed, I embrace the opportunity because I have a post ready. Guest posts help you gain a wider audience for your own blog and readership for books you publish in the future.

Study your blog performance. Collecting and analyzing data about your blog performance will guide you in producing a better blog. For example, I get the most readers, comments, and shares when my posts are between 600-1,000 words.

Book Reviews

Good writers generally love to read. Reading books in our area of expertise or in the fiction genre in which we write strengthens our knowledge base and offers us clear examples of what to do or what not to do in our own writing. Reading books is a good practice for all writers.

Writing reviews for the books you read is better. Book reviews are not like the old book reports you did in school. A good book review is specific as to why the reader liked or disliked the book and is often used by other readers as a gauge in whether or not to purchase the book. Reviews can be powerful.

Remember, however, a review is only strong if it is well written and specific in detail without giving the story away (translate: avoid spoilers). To write a meaningful book review you need to be concise. You must make every word count. You need to come up with a title for your review. You need to self-edit your work before posting. Book reviews are great exercises for both fiction and nonfiction writers.

I suggest you go to Goodreads or Amazon and find a book you've read or want to read. Read through the reviews. Mark yes to the ones you find helpful. Go back and re-read those. What is it that you liked? What made you think these particular reviews were helpful in deciding whether or not to purchase or read the book? Look for common factors. On Goodreads, you can type in the titles of your favorite books and write reviews for them even if you read them last year. You will be helping the authors who crafted the work while you learn and grow as a writer. I try to write at least one review every month.

Notes:

Your Exercise Assignments: I'm giving you three. Of course there are many more opportunities. Keep your eyes and ears open and know that every time you write, you are improving your game.

1.   In the space below, write a paragraph featuring at least two members of your family.

2.   Write a true story about your cat, dog, or Christmas. (I chose these topics because they are part of the *Chicken Soup for the Soul* collection every year.)

3. Do a quick search of writing contests on the internet. Choose one and briefly list the contest guidelines below.

Edit...The Second Big "E"

Whenever I talk about editing to novice writers, they tend to head down a path I'll call mechanics: spelling and grammar. I have actually had adults tell me there shouldn't be a need for professional editors now that we have spellcheck and grammar check built into the word processing systems. That is being naïve.

Hone your editing skills. You can't take the place of hiring a professional editor for your final manuscript—in fact, I know many editors who also write and they hire outside editors for their novels. Why? No matter who you are, you can be so close to your work, you will miss even glaring edits or developmental issues. However, learning to self-edit will save you time, money, and frustration, not to mention a modicum of embarrassment. A writer friend of mine once explained it this way, "You don't want to have your character pet the cat in chapter five when the cat died in chapter three and you forgot."

You may miss a few such quirks, but your readers won't. Do all you can to achieve accuracy and consistency. Do all you can to achieve clarity and error-free writing. Then turn it all over to a professional editor and see what you missed.

In order to address what you can do to develop those self-editing skills, it is important we talk about a few of the different types of editing. Understanding these will help you systematically work through your own manuscript.

Developmental or Structural Editing

I must start this section by saying there is no replacement for hiring a developmental editor. A developmental editor or structural editor looks at your manuscript as a whole. Presenting your writing in a consistent, meaningful way makes your writing stand out. This is true for both nonfiction and fiction writing. The facts must add up.

The arguments made in a persuasive essay, like the actions of the character in a novel, must make sense.

That said, enlist beta readers and critique groups to help you catch discrepancies before you hire a professional editor. A writer working from an outline can compare the completed project with the projected plan. If you have written a proposal or synopsis for your manuscript you can use that as a measure for the writing completed. I once read a research report for a teacher education program that didn't match the premise stated in the abstract. The writers of the report had divided the work. The person drafting the abstract wrote it based on the early discussions and not on the final research findings. It was bad.

Line Editing

Line editing is a sentence-by-sentence look at your manuscript. During this phase of editing, you are looking at grammar, punctuation, spelling, word usage, and clarity. Much of what you need to fix can be revealed using these two tools: read your manuscript out loud and use the search feature on your word processing program. Here are some suggestions for employing these two tools to improve the quality of your writing.

1. Look for overused words or phrases. To do this, use the search feature. I remember being at a writing retreat when one author laughed out loud and announced, "I must love the word 'shrugged.' My characters are shrugging all over the place! 'he shrugged', 'she shrugged', 'the girl shrugged'. I need a new dialogue tag!" If you notice you tend to overuse certain words, complete a word search to see how often they show up in your manuscript. I often first notice these when, like my author friend, I read a chapter out loud.
2. Look for run-on sentences. An easy way to find these is to read your manuscript out loud. As you run out of breath, you'll find those crazy run-ons that should be recast.

Interestingly enough, shorter sentences actually increase the pace of your manuscript. It is a win-win.
3. Reading your manuscript out loud will help you identify awkward sentences or phrases as well. I have worked with writers who, in reading their work out loud "read" what they intended to say instead of what is on the paper. It is important to read word for word. That is how you will find the errors and complicated or confusing sentences and phrases.
4. You want your words to count. We all fall into the weak word pit from time-to-time. Words such as "very", "really", and "just" do not add value to our work. To avoid the use of weak words, keep a list. Search your manuscript for those weak words you tend to use. You can read more about weak words on the internet. Searching the topic will also show you how many authors recognize this pitfall and how they work to overcome it.
5. The last issue to address in line editing at this level is the overuse of adverbs. Search your document for them. Though we use adverbs in our everyday speech, adverbs weaken your writing. A simple search for words ending in "l-y" will help you locate adverbs. Read the sentence and see if you can show the emotion or intensity of the action in that sentence using a different word or structure.

Copyediting

In crafting a novel, copyeditors attend to formatting and style, as well as catching errors in spelling, punctuation, and grammar sometimes missed by others during the process.

I tend to type "form" instead of "from." Spellcheck won't catch that error. I have also noticed others miss it when I use "form". I don't know if it is because they are using the context of the sentence or if our eyes play tricks on us. I know it is a problem area for me. There are a couple of ways I can check my manuscript. I can search "form" to make sure I didn't mean "from" in the sentence or I can take a printed copy and read the text backwards. This helps me catch other spelling errors.

Make sure your punctuation is consistent. I sat in a room with twenty-two English teachers and listened in as they tried to agree on the use of a comma in a particular passage. Be consistent. When your publisher assigns a copyeditor to your work, they will make changes if necessary to fit that publisher's standards. Copy editors will also find issues with internal consistency. Remember the cat that died in chapter three?

As for grammar, again, reading the manuscript out loud is extremely helpful in catching grammatical errors.

Certainly there are other types of editing. The purpose here is to alert you to strategies you can employ prior to submitting your document for publication. Getting into the habit of combing through your writing to strengthen the wording, fix grammatical or spelling errors, and to ensure clarity and consistency throughout will make your manuscript shine.

Your assignment: Jump on the internet and search for "weak words in writing." Take a look at your own writing. Find new ways to say what you need to say without using any of the words you should avoid. Write five words from the list you think pop up in your writing below. Hint: I keep such a list posted above my desk of words to avoid, including adverbs.

Educate. Yep, the Learning Never Stops

One of the best habits you can develop as a writer is engaging in learning activities to strengthen your craft. The person who thinks he or she has it all down and need never learn anything new about writing is headed for failure. Learning new techniques, styles, trends, technologies, and requirements of the industry is a large part of the professional development of every author.

Let's take a look at four topics relevant to pursuing your writing career and ways to learn more in each area. This will be an ongoing endeavor. Education is never a "one and done" proposition. The specific areas discussed here fall under these four umbrellas: how to write, how to research, how to publish, and how to market.

How to Write

You want to write. You may be asking yourself, "How do I even begin to write a novel?" Or your question could be how to write a blog or an article, a book proposal or a query letter.

Your "how to write" question may take the form of genre:

- How do I write historical fiction?
- What are the necessary elements in writing a romance?
- What's the difference between mystery and suspense?
- What are the rules regarding writing a biography?
- How do I write for young adults or for children?

Your own "how to write" question may be specific to a journal or textbook publisher. In this case you may start with the journal's submission guidelines or by reviewing the titles of various publishers to see if your work fits their offerings.

You can often learn the answers to these questions by reading a book or blog, joining a writing group, signing up for a webinar, working with a mentor, or heading to your local library for some serious research. You may want to look at course offerings at your local community college or online courses to help you in your quest.

One place to learn about any "how to write" question is at a writing conference. I have attended conferences focused on fiction as well as conferences addressing nonfiction writing for both full-length books and freelance writing. I will address getting the most out of a conference a bit later. For now, do this:

Your assignment: Identify the questions you are asking. List at least three possible ways to educate yourself on the topic.

How to Research

I've heard writers say, "I write fiction. I don't research." Guess what? Everyone, even authors creating a fantasy world, engages in research. "How could this work?" "What does this mean?" "Is there a precedent for this?"

How do you learn research skills? Develop a plan. I often use what some refer to as the "rabbit trail" method. I start by searching my topic on the internet. This gives me key words and an overview of the topic. My next level of research is to talk with people in the field. I attend conferences where people are explaining new research tools or ways to use what we have in new ways. For example, I attended a workshop where an author demonstrated how she used Google maps to familiarize herself with a geographic location she wanted to include in her book.

Here is an example from my debut novel, *Breathing on Her Own*. One of my characters was in trouble. She was being sued. This was a high stakes case. Laney and her family could lose everything. The story took place in Ohio, so I researched everything I could find on civil suits in Ohio. I talked with lawyers and read a few actual cases. I talked with a friend who owned an insurance company. I needed to know how much insurance Laney probably carried, how the lawsuit might affect the insurance payout, and so forth. You get the idea.

For nonfiction works, I use the same process. I start with a search on the internet. I do not take everything I read on the internet as definitive. I also do not rely on any one method. For example, I was asked to write a freelance piece for *Home Health Aide Digest* on the effects of alcohol on a client's mental and emotional health. The many variables such as age, PTSD, and other medications, required I dig deeper than what was available on the internet.

Writing tip: Don't let your research overshadow writing your first draft. When you come to a question you need to research, write it down or highlight the section. Do not interrupt the flow of writing to answer the question. You will conduct your research and include your findings in your second or third draft.

> **Learning to research needs to be part of every writer's toolkit.**

How to Publish

Should I publish my work myself or go with a traditional publisher? How do I pitch my concept to an agent or acquisitions editor? How do I read a contract? These are legitimate questions writers need to pursue. It is part of our publishing education.

One of the resources I recommend is the *Writer's Market*. This annual publication will give you valuable information on publishers, trends in the market and guidelines for publishing.

Many authors are choosing to take on the publishing work themselves. What used to be scoffed at as vanity publishing or self-publishing is now a far more respectable venture for some authors. The more acceptable term for people taking the independent route to publication is indie authors. I highly recommend the book *A.P.E.: Authors, Publishers and Entrepreneurs- How to Publish a Book,* by Guy Kawasaki and Shawn Welsh, if you want to understand the indie publishing business. I also highly recommend you hire a professional editor if you decide to indie publish. The Kawasaki book will help you understand the traditional route as well. In your how-to-publish quest, be sure to research beyond the big publishing houses. Check out midsized and small presses. You don't want to submit your cozy mystery to someone who only publishes fantasy and science fiction.

How to Market

One of the areas you will need to study as a writer is how to market your article, short story, novel, or nonfiction piece. You will even need to know how to market yourself as a writer. You need to collect information on these topics as you write. Begin reading articles and blog posts about marketing. It is helpful to note ways others are marketing themselves and their materials so you can see what you like and don't like.

In the Part 3 of this book, Marketing You and Your Writing, we will explore the details of how to market yourself as a writer. One of those marketing pieces includes the use of social media. If you have not already done so, you will want to consider signing up with Facebook, Twitter, Pinterest, Instagram, or one of the ever-emerging social media options. Research them. You do not need to participate in all of them. Find one or two you like and focus on those. I use Facebook and Twitter. One of my daughters is a fan of Instagram. I have an author friend who enjoys Pinterest. Connecting with others is the focus. Your understanding of how to market will include how to use social networks effectively.

The publishing industry has changed. As I stated earlier, no longer do publishers send their authors out on tours. While book signings may still draw a few readers to a brick-and-mortar bookstore, you need to learn effective ways to use online resources to draw attention to your work.

I recently met a man at church who teaches a mid-week class at the church. The class is based on a book he wrote about the early Christian church. He told me he hates marketing so he doesn't get involved in it at all. The laughable part of this is that in the six minutes we were together, he invited me to his class, told me about his book, handed me a business card with the book on one side and his contact info on the other and shared that a sequel would be coming out soon on Amazon. He may say he hates marketing, but he was a natural at it.

Learning a bit about marketing will help you in the future when you publish. When *Breathing on Her Own* was released, I was naïve. I assumed my publisher would do everything and I would sit back and rake in the money, offering a television appearance every now and then. Right. I quickly learned I share in the responsibility to market my work.

Now as I write, if I pen a sentence I love, I copy it into a potential quotes file. I can't help but think about pictures and artifacts I come across relating to my story. I've learned how those items may serve in marketing my current work in progress. I learned some of that through experience. Most of it I learned by being a deliberate student of marketing strategies. One purpose of the education piece is to learn about marketing. Don't dwell on it, but when you see an article in *Writer's Digest* or read a blog post on the subject, you are engaged in your work as a writer.

Eventually, you will not only study marketing, you will be marketing. Later in this text you will begin to build a marketing plan. For now, know it is out there and will be something you will need to learn.

Assignment: Create a list of what you need to research, questions you have about writing, publishing, content, or anything else that comes to mind. When you bump into an unknown word or phrase while talking with another author, ask. Learn. Grow.

Engage with Others in the Writing Community

For this portion of the book, I want to first address the topic of writing conferences. Specifically, we'll look at what to do before, during and after a writing conference. Much is available to you on the use of social media to engage with the writing community and with your readers, so later in this chapter I will review ways to engage with those tools briefly.

Conferences

Before the conference:

1. Set three goals for the conference: For example, I set one goal to meet five writers in my genre. A second goal is to pitch my story to an agent or acquisitions editor. The third goal is to learn everything I can about crafting suspense novels. (Yes, these were actual goals I set for a conference in 2015.)
2. Research the workshops carefully. Make sure the choices you make fit your business plan we will develop in the Part 2 of this book.
3. Prepare materials: business cards to share with other participants, editors, agents and so forth. A current trend is to create a "one-sheet." A one-sheet is, in essence, a visually appealing sell sheet for your book. We'll discuss details on constructing a one-sheet in the marketing section, but for now, think of it as full color ad for your book. It will have a compelling image relating to the story or character. It will have a blurb about your book and a tagline. The one-sheet will also feature your headshot, your contact information, and your writing credentials. If you have an agent, you will also include that information. Don't have enough to build one yet? Don't worry about it. I met one woman at a conference who prepared a half sheet with her name, contact info, and a brief bio. She was ahead of me. My attempt at a one-sheet for a book I was hoping to

publish looked like a real estate ad with me as the listing agent. I didn't use it at all.
4. Before you leave home to attend the conference, study the bios of the faculty/administrators/ agents, editors and publishers attending. Learn their specialties; if the bio says they are not accepting Amish stories, don't make an appointment with them to pitch your Amish vampire bride series to them, even if you think it is more vampire than Amish. Research their publishing houses and the titles they have put out in the past year or two. Look to see how many titles they publish each year. Learn everything you can about them. Research the agents. Who do they represent? What publishing houses do they work with on a regular basis? How do they accept submissions? Look at their websites. Study their profiles. Read the bios of the faculty presenting workshops. Research their credentials. What expertise do they have in the field?
5. Practice your elevator pitch if you have a manuscript. An elevator pitch is a well-rehearsed thirty-second pitch to convince someone they should be interested in your manuscript. The idea is this: if you entered an elevator with a premier agent or publisher and the door closed, you have thirty seconds to tell that person about your work and convince them to take a chance on you and your manuscript. And remember, it is always best to have a completed manuscript before you pitch if you have never been published. The acquisition editors may ask you to send a complete manuscript to them. If you don't have a completed work and they have to wait a few months, they will likely forget you and lose interest in your writing.
6. Practice your interviewing skills. What do you want to make sure they know about you and your writing? Learn how to give the information you want them to know, regardless of the question asked.

<u>During the conference:</u>

1. Writing conferences are as much about networking as they are about honing your craft. During the conference,

exchange business cards with other conference attendees and presenters. Make note on the back of their card something you talked about or where you met or something memorable. You'll need that information later.
2. Take meticulous notes during workshops, speaker presentations, and conversations with editors, publishers, and critique groups. I take time each evening of the conference to review the notes and add missing information or formulate questions to ask of the presenter or other conference attendees the following day.
3. Stay hydrated and get rest.

After the conference:

Step 1: One of your first tasks is to email each professional you met at the conference. If you met with agents, acquisition editors, or representatives from anyone in the industry, send them a thank you. Thank each for meeting with you, making a specific reference to something you discussed ("Thank you for the time you took to discuss the potential market for my devotional book, *Songs for the Summer*, at the XYZ Writer's Conference this past weekend.").

It is acceptable to send this via email. If you have a snail mail address, send a handwritten note. You won't always have access to those addresses, but when you do, a handwritten note sets you apart from other attendees.

Remember those contact cards you collected from other conferees? Be sure to email those people as well. You want the recipient to remember where and when you met. Be as specific as possible. Your email can be as brief as, "Hi Pat, it was great meeting you at the XYZ writing conference last week. Thanks so much for the blogging tips you offered over lunch. I look forward to hearing how your book on rooftop gardening turns out. "

Invite them to join you on Facebook or Twitter. If you have a blog or website, be sure to give them your online addresses for these as well. Add to your conference notes a section about the people you met and any details you remember about them. Include their contact info in your notes.

Step 2: Get a massage or whatever you need to do to unwind.

Step 3: After the massage, take time to go through the notes you took at the conference. I type my notes up and keep a spreadsheet linking the notes to keywords. Why should you do this? Months or even years later, you will run into a question begging for an answer. You will vaguely remember hearing something about that sometime, somewhere. I know. I've lived this life. Searching my handwritten notes is time-consuming. My simple Excel spreadsheet is easy to use. I have a column for the name of the session, one for the presenter, one for his or her contact info, columns for key words, and a place for a brief description. I also include the date and venue and the name of the file where I can find my notes. I file mine by the conference name and date.

File your typed notes by conference or topic. You can keep them in a Word file on your computer, print them, or send them to your cloud. You do what works for you. I generally print out my notes as well and attach them to any handouts from the sessions I attended. Now I can search my spreadsheet for a keyword and know exactly where to find the notes and handouts.

The conference has likely broadened your perspectives about your writing. This is the time to revisit the business plan you will create in the Part 2 of this book. Does your plan reflect who you really are or want to be as a writer? Have you clearly stated your goals? Have your writing goals changed?

Examine your business plan carefully. Look for any holes. For example, although I had considered blogging, I did not realize the importance of using this tool as a platform until I attended my first conference. I identified this as a hole in my business plan.

Once you have found an area you need to address, formulate a plan to fix it. For me, I decided to read several other writers' blogs to identify what types of content I needed and what appealed to me as a user. I then researched blogging and found an online tutorial to help me develop a plan to implement my blog. I didn't want to launch the blog until I finished the tutorial, so I decided to begin writing a weekly entry on my existing Facebook page. I took this route so I could develop the habit of regular online writing I would need as a blogger.

If you have fully engaged in the conference, you have learned more about yourself and what you can or should do. Revise your timeline to realistically meet your goals.

Engaging With Others Using Social Media

I love people. I love talking with them, socializing, and sharing life experiences. I have friends from work, school, and church. Connecting with people face-to-face? No problem.

As an author, I have to connect with people outside my circle of friends. Social media helps me do that. I am not going to get into the specifics of all of the social media available. In all likelihood it will all change tomorrow. Instead, I will address a few issues important to writers regardless of the media source used.

First you need to separate your personal life from your professional life. I maintain a Facebook page for my personal life. Of course I have writer friends and connections to publishers and editors through that page, but I also have a Facebook page for my presence as an author. I invite people to "like" that page and I try to post information pertinent to writing, authors, books, and so forth. My author page is linked to my Twitter account so that my posts on my author page show up as tweets. That's good. I get more bang for my buck. I wouldn't want to have every post I place on my personal page show up on Twitter. That would be, as my son-in-law would say, "TMI," too much information.

Second, make sure your name and profile are similar on all social media accounts pertaining to your writing. My Facebook author account is **Rebecca Waters Author** and my Twitter handle is **@WatersAuthor**. I want it to be easy for people to find me. This is part of establishing your brand.

Third, be sure to post regularly on the social media accounts you use. This can be time-consuming to do daily. That's why I use one of the free applications to schedule my tweets and I link my Facebook author page to my Twitter account. I can schedule my Facebook posts as well. I often sit down one day a week to schedule most of my tweets and posts for the week. When I know I'm going to have a busy week or month, I'll schedule accordingly. I still check my accounts regularly, commenting, liking, re-tweeting and so forth. Remember, it is still a *social* connection. You will hurt yourself if you think it is a one-way delivery system, which brings us to the next point.

Fourth, use the eighty-twenty rule. Eighty percent of your online professional communication should be about other people, writing in general, quotes, notifications for the common good and so forth. Only twenty percent (or less) should be about you, your books, or your successes.

Fifth, start somewhere. You don't have to have a presence on every social media site. Choose the ones you feel comfortable using and can maintain with regularity.

Your assignment for Engaging With Others: Research conferences in your genre or area of interest. Find out about the cost, the topics, and the resources. Most conferences are cyclical. If you can't go to one or attend online, it will likely be available next year or the year following.

List your top three picks. Write down the location and a note about what attracts you to that conference.

The Final "E"...Evaluate

You need to take time on a regular basis to evaluate where you are and where you are headed. Review your business plan. We'll develop your business plan in Part II. For now, put it in your mind that it is not a one and done piece. Look at your goals and objectives. Revise them if necessary or draft new ones to reflect where you are in the process.

I revisit my plan the last week of February. At that time I review my mission/vision statement. Does it still reflect who I am and how I want my work to be viewed? I re-examine my strengths and weaknesses and goals and objectives to address them. Which ones have I met? Where do I go from here? What else might I include?

The budget I drafted in my business plan has likely changed. (Let's hope it's for the better.) I need to assess my current needs and plan accordingly.

Here is an example of how revisiting and evaluating your business plan helps you to move forward with your writing.

After my husband died, my writing came to a stall. I had a hard time focusing on any project. The second year following Tom's death, I reviewed my plan and decided I needed to focus on my writing. I needed to slow down and not put myself under the pressure of connecting with an editor or agent. I needed to connect with my craft. I needed to rekindle my desire to write and find affirmation that I was on the right track. I thought about skipping a conference for the year until I happened on a small one in Michigan, led by writers, for writers. There was no expectation to pitch my book. The focus was on improving my craft. It was exactly what I needed. Moreover, it aligned with my plan to address my weaknesses and the two-day format fit both my schedule and my budget.

I also review my business plan when I feel stuck or suffer from writer's block. It is a way for me to re-evaluate where I am and where I am going. I evaluate my strengths and weaknesses before attending a conference or signing up for a webinar. I want to get the most out of every opportunity.

Evaluating takes another form. I am constantly evaluating my writing. I can do this by engaging in a critique group that will offer feedback or work with a beta reader for my completed manuscript. I don't have to take their advice, but they offer me a framework for self-evaluation. I want to grow as a writer. I try to learn from comments made.

Ask yourself these questions:

- In what ways am I a stronger writer than I was last year at this time?

- What seems to be the biggest stumbling block keeping me from moving forward in my writing career?

- What action am I willing to commit to doing to overcome obstacles in my way?

Your assignment: Write a letter to your future self. In this letter, write down what you sensed was your biggest stumbling block to achieving your dream. Write down at least two ways you pursued to overcome it.

Part II Designing a Business Plan for Your Writing

You are writing. Good for you. Now you are ready to design a business plan. A business plan sounds like a manufacturing company or a storefront making and selling widgets. I suppose in a way that's what you are doing. You are the designer, manufacturer, and lead sales rep for your writing business. It makes sense to have a roadmap to get you to your destination.

Getting Started
What do you want from writing?
You're a writer. Or you want to be one. It doesn't matter if you have written a short story for your high school newspaper, a novel, or a love letter to that special someone. Something inside of you told you to pick up this book and learn how to make your writing work for you.

Answer this question: What do you want from writing?

Do you want a career to financially support you and your family?
Do you want to be famous?
Do you want to be a freelance writer?
Do you have a story in you that captures your imagination?
Do you want to write fiction?
Do you want to write novels, short stories, screenplays or poetry?
Are you an expert in your field and you want to write non-fiction works to share your knowledge?
Do you want to write a blog?

And, as if that isn't enough, ask yourself these questions:

Who is your audience?
Do you want to self-publish or be traditionally published?
What do you already know about writing?

Answering these questions will address how you view your work as a writer.

By the way, don't be distraught if you find yourself wanting to do it all! That would be me. I want it all. I suspect I am not alone. There are many of us out there.

Curiously enough, making money and becoming famous are the top two responses I hear from would-be authors. They are also the most elusive.

A business plan for writers:
There are several types of business plans. Some plans are drafted as personal plans, while others are developed for corporations. The purpose of some business plans is to secure investors while others inform stakeholders of the growth development and future plans of the organization.

Let's consider your writing as your business. You are self-employed. Do you have stakeholders? Yes. And no. Your agent is someone willing to invest in you. Your editor or publisher is willing to invest in you. However, you are your main stakeholder until you get the work done.

A business plan is not a completely foreign concept for most successful writers. Those writers developing a proposal for a book or writers preparing a query for a periodical will readily recognize the elements of a corporate business plan as they apply to a specific work-in-progress (WIP).

If you are writing a book to publish, you will take elements of this book in a different direction when it comes to the publication of your work—even generate a business plan for your book.

Why have a business plan for your writing?
A plan helps you succeed at your business. Moreover, having a plan helps you as you write. Consider these points:

1) A business plan will help you remain focused on your mission.
2) A business plan will guide you to "the next step" when you feel overwhelmed and uncertain.
3) A business plan will remind you of your goals and how to reach them.
4) A business plan will help you evaluate the value of a "must have" book or marketing tool being pitched to you.
5) In short, a business plan will help you reach your goal: to publish or share your writing with others.

Topics covered in this section:
Defining and refining your vision or mission as a writer
Identifying your strengths and weaknesses
Budgeting your time and money
Engaging with others in the writing and publishing community

Engaging with Part II:
Each section of Part II covers an essential element for developing your business plan. I suggest you go through each portion in the order they are presented, completing the exercises at the end of each. Once you have completed all of the exercises, I will guide you in putting it all together in a way that is meaningful to you. This will be a usable draft plan you can use to launch your writing career.

Your business plan is both a static and dynamic document.
Static, in that it serves to keep you anchored and focused as you write. Dynamic, in that it is a plan that will evolve even as you change and grow as a writer.

My Story

In many ways I have thought of myself as a writer since I was in second grade. My second grade teacher liked a creative piece I wrote as a class assignment. She had it published in our school newspaper. It was pretty big deal since the school was large and had classes through the eighth grade. My teacher told me I was a writer.

When I was a senior in high school, a substitute teacher came to take our English teacher's place for a semester. She was good enough as a teacher, but what impressed me the most was the fact she was a published author. She loved writing, so our class did more writing that semester than we had completed in our three previous years of high school.

Upon the completion of one of our early assignments, she pulled my essay from the pile and used it as an example for the class. I beamed when I saw the A+ on the top of the paper. As she handed it to me she said, "You are a writer."

You would think with that sort of affirmation coming from my teachers, I would want to study to be a writer. No. I was already a writer. They told me so. I wanted to be a teacher. I wanted to affirm and encourage children the way my teachers encouraged me.

I was a mom. I wrote stories for my children.
I was a teacher. I wrote stories for my students.
I became a professor at a small Christian university. I wrote research reports, education programs, and professional articles for journals in my field.

In the fall of 2011, following a series of heart issues, my husband had quadruple bypass surgery. He was not overweight. He exercised by riding his bicycle daily. He did not have high cholesterol. At his follow-up appointment that December, his heart surgeon looked him in the eye and said, "It's genetic. It will happen again."

On our drive home from her office, we planned our early retirement. We decided to retire the last day of December 2012. One year. One year to plan what we would do with our time, money, and talents. Okay, mostly our time.

Tom was a research scientist. He decided to keep his hand in his work only in as far as it was needed to complete current projects, speak or teach the odd class here and there, and act as a consultant. Mostly, he wanted to move to Florida where we grew up and spend his days fishing or on the golf course.

I was the chair of the education department at the university. The work was both challenging and rewarding. I considered teaching an online course but quickly dismissed the idea. I thought about offering my services as a consultant for teacher education programs but couldn't see how I could give it my all if I spent seven months of the year in one state and five in another, or traveling.

I prayed about what God would have me do. My husband encouraged me to use the time to pursue my dreams. "Why don't you publish some of your children's books?" he asked. It was worth considering. If not children's books, then maybe articles on education or a novel. I was all over the board with possibilities.

In February of 2012, I announced I had decided to become a published author. I didn't know yet what I would write, but I would be a writer. The first week of March was Spring Break. I used the time to draft a business plan for becoming a writer. Much of what I researched and learned through that process is in this book. I have presented on the topic to writers groups. I have published the information on my blog and created articles from it for guest posts. I have guided fellow writers, both new and seasoned, in developing their own business plan. I can do this with confidence because I attribute the successes I experience as a writer to both God and the plan.

My first book, *Breathing on Her Own*, was released the last week of March 2014. In October of 2014, my husband was in a bicycling accident. Within two hours of the accident, Tom died. My world was shattered. Writing? It was not on my to-do list. Try to breathe. Survive. Manage. Those were my only goals for 2015.

I was scheduled to attend a writing conference in September of 2015. In August I decided if I was going to pursue writing as a career, I needed to attend the conference. I wasn't ready. I needed to get back to my writing. If you are a writer, you know how hard it can be to return to the daily process of writing after a significant amount of time away.

I turned to my business plan. I reviewed my goals and objectives. I took stock of my projects. This rekindled an interest in what I was doing. I decided I could not return to the project I had been working on when Tom died. He was too much a part of it. I turned to the editing of one completed manuscript and reviewed the synopsis for another project I had in mind. I launched into my writing with renewed energy. By the time I left for the conference, I had one complete manuscript fully edited and was two-thirds of the way through another book.

The business plan served as a guide for my next steps in writing. It also helped me choose the workshops most beneficial to helping me reach my goals.

That is my story. Are you ready to write yours? To take the next step in your writing career? Here we go!

Identifying Your Strengths and Weaknesses

Strengths and weaknesses. We all have them.
In this section you will identify (or at least begin to identify) your strengths and weaknesses as a writer. You will begin to outline a plan to build on your strengths and address your weaknesses.

This requires some thoughtful **self-examination**. For example, I identified my weaknesses in understanding and engaging in social media networks. Since research is one of my strengths, I created a plan that included learning everything I could about Facebook and Twitter. Eventually, I set up a Twitter account and launched an author page on Facebook.

I asked some of my writer friends to identify their strengths and weaknesses. The list may help you in thinking about your own writing, but don't let it overwhelm you. I offer it only as a prompt for a few areas you may want to consider.

Here are the weaknesses they identified…and remember, many of these are published, successful authors!

- Grammar
- Point of View
- Overuse of weak words (just, really, felt, etc.)
- Marketing
- Technology
- Tend to "tell" instead of "show"
- Writing natural-sounding dialogue
- Overuse of adverbs
- How to write a query
- How to pitch to an agent or editor
- Self-editing
- Plotting
- Sagging middle
- Editing/revising

Notes:

Here are a few of the strengths they identified:

- Technology
- Grammar
- Dialogue
- Plot development
- Editing/revising
- Research

Notice that many of the same elements were identified by at least one writer as a strength while others said it was a definite weakness. Also, look at the number of weaknesses. More than twice as many weaknesses as strengths!

Notes:

Writing to Publish: Part II

Assignment: This is a two-part assignment. In one column, list your strengths and in the other, your weaknesses. Try to limit yourself to no more than <u>five</u> strengths and no more than <u>three</u> weaknesses. You don't want to feel inadequate or overwhelmed before you start! *And* I don't want you bouncing around with an overinflated ego. You'll spin out of control at your first rejection.

Strengths   Weaknesses

1.   1.

2.   2.

3.   3.

4

5.

For part two of this assignment, I want you to write a sentence for each strength you listed, stating how you can use those strengths to your advantage.

I shared that research is one of my strengths. Here is another example. Renee-Ann Giggie, author of *Stella's Plea,* is an interpreter for the deaf. She has worked with people in the deaf community for many years. When she decided to write a novel, she drew on her knowledge of the deaf culture. The kidnapped child in *Stella's Plea* is a deaf girl. She incorporated her strength in developing both an interesting character and a conflict in her plot, often identified by writers as weak areas.

For each weakness, I want you to write down *at least* two ways to address it. Here are two examples:

Example 1: "I worry my grammar isn't good enough."

Possible ways to address it:
    1. Get a book on grammar usage at the library
    2. Read a NYT best seller every week.
    3. Take a course at my local community college on writing
    4. Join an online critique group

Example 2: I often get on the computer intending to write, but I get distracted by social media and games, so I waste a lot of time.

Possible ways to address it:
    1. I will set aside one hour every morning before breakfast to write and reward myself at the end of the hour with free time on the computer.
    2. I will write 500 words a day before I play any computer games.
    3. I will join a writing group for accountability.

I think you get the idea. Study your own list carefully. Determine what possibilities are before you. A caution here. Make sure your solutions are within your reach. Yes, it would be wonderful to say "I'll write 1,000 words every morning before I do anything else," but that may not be within your reach. However, you may achieve the same outcome by saying "I'll write 500 words in the morning and 500 words at night." For me, that is achievable and far more realistic.

Your turn:

Selecting Your Goals and Objectives

Now is the time to set **goals** for your writing. Let's take a close look at goals and objectives. An important step in creating your business plan is to identify specific goals and objectives. Without a long-range goal and several smaller, short-term objectives you will struggle to make writing a priority. You will wander about aimlessly, talking at parties about the book you want to write …someday.

In this section you will learn how to write out long-range goals and short-term objectives. You will learn how to make sure your goals and objectives are specific and attainable.

Setting a goal to write a novel in the next three months is reasonable for me. If I were still teaching at the university full time, though, I would need to extend that time frame. One possible short-term objective to reach that goal might be, "I will write an average of 1,000 words a day, six days a week."

Setting your goals. One acronym used by many to work through the process of creating goals is called SMART: S̲pecific, M̲easurable, A̲ttainable, R̲ealistic, and T̲ime-bound. Let's take a look at how that works for our business plan as a writer.

S-Specific A goal needs to be specific. For example, I may have a goal to improve my golf game. That is great, but not specific. In what way do I want to improve my game? A more specific goal would be to lower my average golf score or handicap.

Let's put this in terms we might explore as writers. I could say, "I want to write a book." This is not specific. It will not move me any closer to writing a book than saying I want to improve my golf game will get me an invitation to the LPGA. Let's try this one instead: "My goal is to write a short novel." At least I'm heading in the right direction. Let's look at the next component to make that goal stronger.

M-Measurable As well as being specific, your goal needs to be measurable. Stick with me as I go back to my golf game for a moment. I can make this a stronger goal by including a way to measure it. "My goal is to lower my average score by three strokes." Is that measurable? Of course. I can readily see if I have attained my goal by comparing last year's average with this year's scores.

Let's take this back to our writing example. "My goal is to write a 65,000 word short novel." It is specific and measurable. I can readily see my word count daily as I move toward that goal.

A-Attainable My next question is this: "Is this goal attainable?" Is it possible to shave three strokes off my golf score —without using an eraser, mind you? I think it is. It may require spending some serious time working on my putts. If I said I'm going to reduce my score by ten strokes, I would be setting myself up for failure. Three strokes, however, is attainable.

Let's apply this to our writing example. Is writing a 65,000 word novel attainable? Yes. Think about it this way. If I write 500 words a day, I will have my novel written in a little over four months. That is assuming I write every day.

R-Realistic I must be realistic. I may be able to improve my golf game, but I am not going pro. I am able to write a 65,000 word novel in four months, but it is not going to be ready for publication. It is not likely to be a New York Times best seller nor will it be turned into a movie. Those things can happen, but be realistic. A more realistic goal is to say, "My goal is to *draft* a 65,000 word novel." Once finished, I can set a new set of goals for getting it ready for publication.

Also, to be realistic your goal needs to be within your control. I could write a goal to get it published, but that is only in my control if I opt to self-publish. A more realistic goal is to say, "I will submit my manuscript to publishers and/or agents for publication."

T- Time-bound To reach your goal, to be able to measure it, to move forward, you need to make sure your goal is time-bound. Again, be reasonable. In the golf example, I can say, "I will reduce my average golf score by three strokes during the next season with my league." My league runs from May to September. A specific time.

For our writing example we can say, "My goal is to draft a 65,000 word novel over the next six months." Notice that although I pointed out that it is possible to draft the book in just over four months, I've lived this life. I know myself and know I will be involved with other activities as well.

A second goal will be aimed at time spent revising and editing my manuscript. That goal will also need to be specific, measurable, attainable, realistic and time-bound.

I could draft a third goal aimed at taking the steps I need to submit my manuscript for publication.

Now let's look at writing objectives. Objectives are small pieces that will fit together to reach your goal. Objectives should be observable and measurable actions. Think of "observable" as a product of some sort. Evidence. Measurable means you will be able to quantify or assess your success.

Remember that first goal?

Goal: Draft a 65,000 word novel over the next six months.
Here are two possible objectives:
      Objective 1: Write a synopsis of the basic story.
      Objective 2: Write 500 words a day/ five days a week.

Are these objectives observable? Will I have evidence to prove my case for meeting my goal? For Objective 1, I will be able to produce a synopsis. I could show it to you…or an agent, editor, or publisher.

How about Objective 2? Can I produce evidence that I write 500 words a day? I can record my daily word count on a spreadsheet. If asked, I should be able to produce a document that when the math is applied, clearly shows an average of 500 words a day or 2,500 words a week. I doubt I'll be asked for such evidence, but as a writer it is important to think about my objectives as observable and measurable. Otherwise, it is too easy to let your writing fade into the folds of everyday life. If I know I need to have "observable evidence," I hold myself to a higher standard.

I suggest you start with **two goals** for your business plan. In your final business plan, you may extend your goals to include publishing goals, marketing goals, or education goals. <u>Never have more than five goals in your plan.</u> Two to three is the ideal. Too many goals will cause you to feel overwhelmed. Too few and you will quickly lose your vision for being successful as a writer.

Assignment: To get you started, write two goals. Write two to three objectives for each goal.

Identifying Your Mission and Vision

You are now ready to begin drafting your mission and vision statement. This statement reflects who you want to be as writer. When you read a completed business plan, you will see the mission and vision statement at the beginning of the document. To get there, it is best to look at your strengths and weaknesses as well as your goals and objectives *before* crafting your mission or vision piece.

Let's start with your mission. Mission refers to your core purpose or quest. It is, in essence, purpose fueled by conviction. Think Princess Leia in *Star Wars*. You know from the start what she would say is her mission. She follows through with such conviction it leaves your head spinning, right?

So if that is MISSION, what is VISION?

Your vision statement is what you see happening in your writing business in the future. Do you see writing as your primary income? Do you see your name synonymous with "suspense"? "Romance"? If I say the name John Grisham, you likely think legal thriller even though he has written other books.

You are almost ready to draft your mission and vision statement. Almost. For this section, I want you to do the assignment first.

Assignment 1: An effective way to capture your mission or vision statement for your writing is to write a brief obituary for yourself. Don't scowl…and don't laugh. And by all means, stop rolling your eyes! This is actually a very good exercise and will help you narrow down what it is you want others to remember about your writing. In fact, you need not write your entire obit, only the paragraph about the writing you left behind. Once you've finished, come back and we'll get on with the rest of the work needed.

Finished? Good. Your obituary doesn't need to be perfect, but it should give you clues to answer these next few questions.

1. What are the CORE VALUES reflected in the obituary you drafted?

2. How might those core values shape you as a writer?

3. What words in your obit might tell the world why you wanted to write in the first place?

4. What writing did you say you left behind? Freelance work? Novels? Short stories? Poetry? Screenplays? Nonfiction? What?

The first two questions address your mission statement. Your mission statement is your anchor. It helps you assess writing opportunities. A new writer asked me what I meant by "core values." By that, I mean what would you NOT DO for the sake of a sale? What life values do you hold so dear you would never compromise on that point? No matter what.

Early in my writing career I interviewed Debby Mayne, a successful writer of Christian romance novels. She was told she could make more money if she wrote romance with steamy sex scenes. She didn't do it. She remained true to her core values as a "clean" writer.

Questions 3 and 4 reflect the vision you have for writing. You may find you are very focused. I have one writer friend who only writes Amish romance, while another friend is driven in her quest to pen Civil War historical fiction.

That said, don't worry if your answer to number 4 is, "I want to write everything!" I still like to write it all. I write both fiction and nonfiction. As a former teacher, I hold a few children's books I crafted near and dear to my heart. One day I hope to publish those as well. But poetry? No. Screenplays? Not yet. Obituaries? Only this one, thank you.

As you can see, it's easy to blur the lines between a mission statement and a vision statement. That's why they are often combined. They tend to flow together and guide you in how you use your time and other resources.

Another way to think about your mission and vision statement is in terms of "branding." In marketing circles, we come to relate a certain product line and its quality based on "branding." I say, "Goodyear," and you think "tires." I say, "DelMonte," and you think "canned fruit." I say, "Mary Higgins Clark," and you think "suspense. If you are true to your mission and vision statement, your brand shows in your writing. Your writing becomes your brand.

I met a writer at a conference whose vision remains to write historical fiction. Discouraged by lack of interest in her work by publishers, she took advice from an agent to write a contemporary romance novel since there was a greater demand for that sort of book. The romance novel got her published. In her case, she was still true to her core values of crafting a "clean read" novel. If her goal was to be a published author, she was true to that piece as well. However, she now questions that decision. Writing to a trend or audience may prove more of a distraction than it is a boost to her writing career. You see, to fulfill the contract, she had to agree to two more romance books. I can't speak for her. I only know I need to write what I need to write. You need to write what you need to write. Be true to yourself.

Like this woman, I was told by a well-respected literary agent that my writing was good and if I would craft an Amish novel, she could sell it. She told me it would be a sure-fire way to get published quickly. The Amish market was huge at the time, but I didn't do it. My vision for my writing precludes me from chasing a market and I don't want to be disrespectful to the Amish by writing something I can only research on the surface.

Get the idea? You've written your obituary. You've answered the four questions. Mull these over. When you're ready, you can take on the last assignment for this section.

Assignment 2 is twofold. <u>First</u>, draft a mission/vision statement for your business plan. It need not be long. A sentence or two will do. Make it your own and don't worry, you can always revise it later. The <u>second</u> part of this assignment is to find a quote you think supports your mission or vision. There are many sites on the internet to search for such a quote if you don't have one in mind.

Having trouble getting started? Try completing one of these sentences starters:
I want to publish…
When people hear my name, I want them to immediately think of…
My mission is to…
The vision I've cast for my writing includes…

Writing to Publish: Part II

Budgeting Your Time and Money

Creating a budget for your business will help you succeed. Include in your plan statements regarding investment of both your TIME and your MONEY. Most people immediately think of money when they hear the word "budget." I understand. That's why we're going to start with the biggest budgeting issue first: TIME.

TIME. We talk about using spare time to write a novel or a collection of short stories. We enter our writing career with great intentions for maintaining a blog or newsletter. Instead, we clutter our lives with social media and entertainment. We tell ourselves we need these outlets to relax. Unwind. Then we tell ourselves we're too tired to write. At least today. We procrastinate. But here, folks, is the secret to a happy, productive, energized life: **The things that make you tired are the things you leave undone.** Clutter in any form and procrastination on a daily basis wear you out.

How much time are you willing to give to the writing, editing, revising, submitting, publishing, and marketing of your work? You may be surprised to learn you don't need to quit your day job. You need not use your vacation time to write or wait until you retire to pursue your dream. Here is the secret: You need only to be consistent in using the time available to you.

You may find there is a certain time of day that is more productive for you. If so, block out a portion of that time to write. You will write more and write better if you schedule a half hour every day to write than if you try to find that magical whole day to yourself that probably doesn't exist. Many well-known authors started with twenty to thirty minutes at the kitchen table on a regular basis.

Here are two examples from my own life. When I was working on my master's degree, I chose the thesis option over the oral exam because it was structured very much like a dissertation. I wanted to eventually pursue a doctoral degree, so the thesis option was the right choice. I was married and had three active daughters. I worked full time as a teacher in the public school and I was active in my church. I did the research for my thesis, but finding time to pull it all together was a challenge.

I lugged my heavy book bag around everywhere I went in hopes of finding time to work on the project. I carried it to my youngest daughter's dance class. I carried it to the swim team practices. I pulled it out a few times while I waited for one of them to emerge from an after school event. I built muscles hefting my research hither and yon. Unfortunately, I didn't get the writing done by carrying the book bag of notes and files with me.

I whined to one of my professors about not having time to do the work. I told her how guilty I felt when I didn't get anything down on paper. She listened. She smiled. She told me to stop carrying the work with me.

Seriously? But what if that magic moment came and I was sitting somewhere without my paper and pen? My mentor told me to sit down and hammer out five pages every night before I went to bed. She said, "Call the time your office hours. Close the door and write." She suggested I might change my mind and trash every word the next day, but the writing would get done faster and better if I blocked a consistent time to write.

She was right. I wrote five pages every school night after my daughters were in bed. While my girls were in their lessons and practices and jumping into the car breathless with the events of their day, I was present. I was a mom. Mom by Day, Scholar by Night. I should have a T-shirt made. I completed the thesis.

The second example comes from completing the writing of my dissertation. The girls were older now. In fact, my oldest was in college. That should have helped. However, by this time, my middle daughter played French horn. She was very good at it. She was one of the youngest members of the Cincinnati Symphony Youth Orchestra. At the same time, she played in the Middletown Youth Orchestra and the Blue Ash Symphony. She tromped her way across the football field every Friday night with a mellophone in her high school marching band. Add to that, my youngest daughter played violin both at school and in the Middletown Youth Orchestra, was a cheerleader, a member of the yearbook staff, president of Students Against Destructive Decisions (S.A.D.D.) and she was active in our church.

The five-pages-a-day plan took me only so far. I needed to assess my schedule and determine what consistent block of time I could devote to the dissertation. The Cincinnati Symphony Youth Orchestra practiced for three hours every Sunday afternoon on the University of Cincinnati campus. Every Sunday I drove my daughter to her practice in the music building, then spent at least two-and-a-half hours at the library. I completed my doctoral work largely on the one-day-a-week plan.

What I hope you see through these examples is that **consistency trumps good intentions.** You'll get more writing done in less time if it is consistent.

Of course there are other strategies you may employ in your plan. Some writers find it helpful to use a word count quota to meet each day of writing. Other writers use a formula called the chunky method. Take a look on the internet and probe the minds of other authors. Do what works for you. The important part is to write. Carve out the time you need to meet your goal. Find what works for you and do it on a consistent basis.

Assignment: Take a long, hard look at your calendar. Is there a time slot you can schedule your writing? Although writing some every day is ideal to get those creative juices going, consistency is the key. Even if you identify only two blocks of time to write each week, you'll find yourself thinking about the next scene or dialogue in your "off hours." You'll be more productive in the long haul.

Identify the time(s) you'll dedicate to writing and write that into your business plan. Also, put them on your calendar. That way you'll be more likely to keep the appointment you made with yourself.

Create a weekly calendar here:

MONEY. There is a story of a woman who decided to be a writer. As the story goes, this would-be author invested in all the gadgetry of the day. She bought a desk and a state of the art typewriter. (Yes, this is a story I heard as a child.) Her husband encouraged her even after the short stories she composed were rejected time and again. One day, he came home from work to find her smiling broadly and waving a check.
"My writing career finally paid off," she said.
"What did you sell?" he asked.
"My typewriter."

I have no idea if that story is true or not. What I do know is that there is a monetary investment in writing to publish. Be thoughtful in how you spend your money, because unless you are the one-in-a-billion to create a New York Times best seller your first try out, the returns on your initial investment will be minimal.

It is up to you as a professional to explore the financial costs involved. In addition to writing materials—a computer, printer, ink cartridges, pens, paper, index cards, and sticky notes—you'll need a professional headshot, business cards, and training in various areas.

You'll find some of that training at professional conferences. There you will also network with other writers, agents, publishers, editors, and writing coaches. You'll find the need for books on your craft, subscriptions to helpful journals in your new profession, and more. If your book takes place in a specific location, you may need travel expenses to research the area.

If your funds are limited, you'll find creative ways to get what you need. You'll make your own business cards. You'll use library resources instead of investing in copies of books you want to study on the craft. You'll find a Groupon coupon to get that snazzy head shot at a fraction of the cost. (I speak from experience.) And… you'll write about places you know, saving travel expenses for a later book.

Part III of this book will guide you through those marketing areas such as creating business cards, getting a headshot, and acquiring the marketing tools you need. For now, create a place for them in your business plan.

Assignment:
For your budget piece, you will want to create two spreadsheets. On the first, list items you think you will need. Beside each item list the approximate cost. The third item is where you propose alternate ways to get what you want. And remember to list the items you already have and the replacement cost when needed. That includes your computer and printer.

Remember, you don't need to make an enormous investment up front. This part of your business plan helps you seize opportune moments. Having prepared a budget may help you put down that $30 book on writing you liked at the bookstore because you're saving to upgrade your computer. If you really want or need the book, see if you can borrow it from the library. If my local library doesn't have the book, they put the title on the request list and call me when they get it. Sometimes my library borrows it from another library in the state. Another option is to see if the book is available as an e-book. E-books are vastly less expensive.

The second spreadsheet will help you track your actual expenditures and income. Create a spreadsheet along the lines of what you find in a checkbook register: Date, Description, Cost/Debit, and Deposit. This will help you track your expenses and the money you take in for the stories, articles, or books you sell. It will help you at tax time.

Eventually, you will want to consider opening a separate checking account for your writing business. Consult your accountant or talk with a financial planner at your bank. If you become a best selling author and make a movie deal for your time travel novel about Albert Einstein and the ninja warriors, you definitely need to keep your professional monies earned separate from your household account.

The Educational Component in Your Plan

It is now time for you to include an educational component in your plan. You have assessed your strengths and identified your weaknesses. You will add a portion in your plan to address those areas needing growth. How you choose to address your weaknesses depends on your needs, your personal learning style, your personality, and your budget of time and money.

Assignment 1: Read three blogs about writing and publishing. If you find one you really enjoy, subscribe. You will reap the benefits.

Conferences as a Part of Your Plan
Your educational component should include planning for a writing conference. You may attend one in person or find a suitable conference online. Conferences can be costly. However, you get a huge bang for your buck. Conferences offer classes on writing, offer panel discussions, and provide multiple networking opportunities. You can learn more in one three- or four-day conference about writing and publishing than you can in months of research on your own.

Assignment:
In Part I of this book, I had you complete an online search of possible writing conferences. Be sure to consider both online conferences as well as in-person experiences. Include in your business plan details of a conference you would like to attend within the next two years. Write out the basic details. Yes, some of the details may change, but you'll be ready. Put the anticipated cost in your budget sheet.

Sounds like an easy assignment, doesn't it? Wait until you see all of the possibilities. You'll find conferences for every genre all over the world. There are conferences for special interest groups, conferences on cruise liners, and conferences in tropical havens lasting a week or more. Most conferences tend to repeat around the same time each year.

Putting Your Plan Together and In Action
You've assessed your strengths and weaknesses. You've made a plan to address those areas where you need help. You've written down your major goals and objectives for your writing career. You've carefully considered the start-up costs and looked for time slots to fulfill your dream. You've started connecting with like-minded people in your field. Now it's time to put your business plan together.

Before we begin, I want to address the dynamic nature of your business plan. This may well be the most important writing you do. Like any good and usable plan, though, it requires updating and revision as you grow and change as an author. I revisit my plan every year. I am often asked to speak for writing groups, community organizations, conferences, and church events. My speaking activity is bound to my writing experiences in many ways. I now have a place for speaking in my business plan.

> **The simple truth:**
> **Your plan will likely change over time,**
> **But without one, you will lack direction.**

No one is going to ask you for your business plan. It is not a requirement to be a writer. It is a tool to help you move from being a writer to being an author. Getting a contract to publish. The plan is intended to serve <u>you</u>. There is no right or wrong way to organize what you have created.

Here is how I set my plan up to help me focus my attention and resources:

1. I put my mission and vision statement in a box as a header for my plan.

2. My goals and objectives for the year are beneath that box. As

well, I post the objectives on a timeline on my wall. I am a visual person and seeing the smaller pieces I need to complete on a day-by-day or week-by-week basis helps me complete my objectives and reach my goals. It is the only part of my plan I print up and hang in my office.

3. Budgeting time. I have a statement in my plan concerning my time and make sure that is reflected in my daily calendar.

4. Budgeting money. I'll be honest here, I don't look at my budget on a regular basis. I refer to it only to make sure I'm on track. Since I opened my author checking account, I generally use the check register to make sure I have the funds needed for a conference or other tools I need. Each year, however, when I review the plan, I review the budget.

5. My strengths and weaknesses are next. These change every year. Or should.

6. This is not a necessity, but in my plan I have a place at the end where I list books or blogs I want to read.

Your Assignment:
1. Make your business plan your own. It doesn't have to be perfect. It needs to be an arrow pointing you in the right direction. Do this assignment on your computer.

2. Below, sketch a visual such as a timeline, graph, chart, and or image to represent your business plan.

Part III Marketing You and Your Writing

I am often asked questions about marketing a book. People throw around terms such as headshot and tagline, or talk of a book launch, social media presence, or a media kit as though everyone is fully aware of what each means for the new author. Many of us learn by doing. We ask questions. Some authors, publishers, and agents understand the newbie status and extend grace to us. They patiently address our questions one at a time. Some expect us to already know what we're doing and ask for our marketing plan.

The part is for all authors. All. Newbies included. For example the very week I was putting the finishing touches on this part of the book, a new author contacted me and asked what a book launch should include. That same day, I was in a writing group where a woman who has published four novels with a traditional publisher asked if any of us knew anything about a media kit. She'd been asked to send her new publisher a zip file with her media kit and was in a quandary. One of the new authors in our group offered to send her info. We are in this together.

A disclaimer here: This is not an all-inclusive marketing guide. With the ever-changing nature of technology, I doubt such an animal exists. This is a guide to answer questions and get you started.

I have divided Part III into two sections. The first are those items you can do now, even if your book is not yet published. Taking care of these few pieces will serve you well and relieve you of stress in the future. The second section describes those marketing tools you will need once you finish writing your novel, memoir, or nonfiction work. The division is deliberate. New writers need not feel overwhelmed with the marketing piece, yet need to know what is on the horizon. I've included checklists to help you maintain your sanity and click off items as you complete them.

To get the most out of this resource, do these three things:

1. Read the book.
2. Create a virtual file where you can begin to collect what you need.
3. Create a real (read: physical) file where you can keep artifacts you like.

Observe what other people in your genre are doing. Observe what people outside your genre are doing. Your virtual file will eventually become your media kit. Your real file will be a source of inspiration for you.

When someone asks me for my headshot or a picture of the cover of my book or my bio, I go to my virtual file. When I need to come up with a fresh idea to present for a speaking engagement or a related artifact to mail to someone, I consult my real file. In this file I keep such items as samples of bookmarks, handouts, advertisements, articles on marketing, and a list of relevant quotes. Before my second book, *Libby's Cuppa Joe,* was published, I came across some small, affordable journals with a cup of coffee pictured on the front. I bought ten. I keep them in the file as giveaways. The key is to know where you have stored your marketing tools and ideas so they are readily available.

Gearing Up: First Impressions

There is an old saying: You only have one chance to make a first impression. You're reading this book because you know part of becoming a published author is getting people to read what you've written. That is, the right people. People other than your mother. To be published, you need agents or editors, and people in the publishing industry to read your words.

Once you have a book published, you will play a role in marketing the book. Your publisher will do some promotions for you and perhaps even advertise your work. But don't count on it. And if you go the indie publishing route, everything will be up to you to do.

> **Writing is work. You are launching a business –a new and exciting career.**

Celebrities write a book and find instant success. They may do little to market their book. Why? They have been marketing themselves for years. They already have a brand, a platform, and a following. People clamor to hear more from them.

If you're known as an expert in your field, you may find an instant audience for your nonfiction book on the biomechanics of lifting. That would have been my husband, Thomas R. Waters. He wouldn't have needed much to market a text on ergonomics. His name and body of research spoke for itself. However, to extend his reach beyond scientists and practitioners, he would have needed to engage in marketing.

In all likelihood, you are neither a celebrity nor an expert in your field. You are like me, a writer with a story to tell. You have a desire to publish. You're working your day job and cranking up your computer at night to tap in words you hope will change the world. If you're a celebrity or an expert in your field, the tools in this book will serve you in reaching your audience.

There is much you can do before you publish. You may stumble a bit along the way. That's okay. This part of the book will help you. I want to assure you, though, that not all is lost if the first impression you make is less than stellar.

Here is a chapter from my life. I hope this gives you hope, if not a laugh.

"I was on campus today and realized it was the last day to register for tuition remission," my sweet husband told me one night as I was washing the dinner plates. "So I signed you up for a class called Children in Groups. It starts tonight."

"Tonight?"

Tom worked at the University of Cincinnati. We often talked about the possibility of me taking a few classes under the tuition remission policy. It made getting a master's degree more affordable. I thought I might take a class in the summer when I wasn't teaching full time. But, tonight? Tom, always the encourager, offered to drive me to campus and help me find my class. It was a start.

That fall, Tom and the girls drove me to campus every Monday. They walked me to my class and were outside the room when I finished. While I was sitting in a lecture, Tom took our daughters to concerts, parks, and plays. Getting my degree this way was bound to be a piece of cake. He drove me to class again for the winter term.

The spring course offerings were published and I carefully searched for classes meeting my criteria: Monday night. The class I chose was also scheduled to meet in Teachers College. That was a bonus. I now knew exactly how to get to Teachers College and decided I could drive myself. I confidently pulled my minivan up to the same gate we used in previous quarters.

"You can't park here," the gatekeeper said.

"We parked here all last quarter," I told her. Tom's car had a staff issued parking permit. I was a lowly student. The kind woman directed me to a parking garage. It involved several twists, turns, and one-way streets. I assured her I understood, but the minute I pulled away from her kiosk I was lost. I stopped several places along the way asking passersby for directions.

Getting to the garage proved to be only half the battle. Once in the garage I had no idea how to get from there to Teachers College. A man pointed through the opening between the concrete barriers to a building behind the garage, across the ravine. "Over there. That's Teachers College."

The exit for the garage was to the east. The building he pointed out was due west. I made my way to the east gate, walked around the four-story garage, through the grass, and across the ravine. I eventually clawed my way up the hill. In a dress. There may have been another way to get there, but I wasn't about to lose sight of that building.

With a great sense of accomplishment I entered the lower doors and started looking for my room number. The room didn't exist. I asked for help. A young woman said, "Oh you need Teachers College. This is Dyer Hall. They're connected. Go through those doors and up the stairs."

By the time I made it to my assigned room I was a good five minutes late. Ugh! I smoothed the skirt of my dress and approached the door. No one was in the room. A sign indicated the class had been moved to MCM 123. I fought back the tears.

An older gentleman pointed me in the direction of McMicken Hall. I finally found the room and the professor invited me in. "We're just going around the room and introducing ourselves," he said. "I asked everyone to tell us their name and why they're taking the course."

Of course the only available desk was on the other side of the room near the front. I sat down as quietly as possible and listened to my classmates.

"I'm so and so and I'm taking the class because I'm working on my doctorate in communications."

"I'm so and so and Dr. K recommended I take this course."

I've always been an advocate of the old adage, honesty is the best policy, so when my turn came, I simply said, "My name is Rebecca Waters and I took this class because it was offered on Monday."

I later learned the professor was weeding people out of the class. You needed a strong background in cultural differences and language or a recommendation from another professor to be in the class. Fortunately, the professor was able to determine I was qualified after class during the forty minutes it took him to help me find my car.

You *can* overcome first impressions. That professor later became my mentor, my advisor, and my advocate.

The lesson here underscores what I said earlier. Always be yourself, do your best writing, follow your dream and everything else will fall into place. Don't let the fear of failure keep you from trying. Oh, and one more thing: Never be afraid to claw your way up a hill when necessary.

> **Be yourself, do your best writing,**
>
> **follow your dream and**
>
> **everything else will fall into place.**

Putting the Face with the Name

A Word About Branding

Before we launch into specifics of how to present yourself, it's important to be confident of the statement you wish to make. You crafted a mission and vision statement for your writing. One way to think about your mission and vision statement is in terms of "branding."

> Purpose accompanied by conviction is your brand.

Market research guru, Kendall Nash of Burke, Inc. helps people think of brand in this way: "Identify what drives and inspires you and what keeps you up at night. That is your brand."

What are your core values? Your core values define you. Your core values are reflected in your brand. For example, at my core I'm not a person who uses what some call colorful language. People reading my books or contacting me to speak know my brand. They expect a "clean read." They know I won't use offensive language when I'm asked to speak.

One way to identify your brand is to complete this sentence: When people hear my name, I want them to immediately think of….

We not only identify with a particular brand, we come to expect certain things of it. We've all put down a book or walked out of a movie, saying about an actor or the director, "That was disappointing. Not what we've come to expect of him." But if the product was true to the actor, director, speaker, or author, we leave satisfied because the performance matched our expectations based on the brand he or she has created. If you are true to your mission and vision statement, your brand will show in your writing.

With branding in mind, let's dive into the topic of putting the face with the name. You can complete much of this immediately. The rest will come later and you'll be ready.

The first time I was asked to write a guest post, the blog's owner, author Cindy Huff, asked me for my headshot, a short bio, and links to my blog, Facebook page, and Twitter handle. She also told me to include my website.

This may not seem overwhelming to you, but I only had two of the items she requested. I had started a blog so I could provide that link and the bio I had written for it.

The Headshot

When Cindy asked me for a headshot, I stood in my living room with my phone and attempted to capture the real me with a selfie. If you have tried this, you already know some of the pitfalls. I was looking up, down, or curiously sideways. Number seventeen was decent, but the pixels on my phone produced a grainy image for the blog.

Don't wait until the last minute. You can get a good headshot now. You will need it. You will need it for publications and publicity. You will also need a headshot for your social media accounts.

A month or so later, my publisher asked me for a headshot for the back cover of my book, so I started calling studios. The sitting fee alone was outside my budget. I learned I also needed to acquire the digital rights to the photo. The studios I contacted offered me a package deal of $300. That may not sound like a lot to you, but since that would eat up the entire balance of what I budgeted to become a writer, I was not a happy camper.

Fortunately, I have connections. I called my daughter in Wisconsin. Within the hour, she emailed me a Groupon coupon for JC Penney's photography studio. For $25, I received three poses in three different outfits, all digital rights, two 8 X 10s, and three 5 X 7s. The $25 included my sitting fee.

Most writing conferences hire a professional photographer to take headshots for participants. These are generally affordable and provide a great way for new writers to get their photo taken and for old timers to update theirs. Note to self: Do not turn old and gray and try to pass yourself off as that brunette on the cover of your latest book.

The Bio

Many times people will ask you for a brief biographical sketch. You will need it if you publish a book, appear on a blog, offer a workshop, or give a keynote address. You will also need it for your website, your Twitter page and your professional Facebook page. In fact, every time you are "featured," you can count on someone asking you for your bio.

Write it now. You will need to update it or rewrite it from time to time as your credentials and interests change, but you will have a place to start if you draft your bio today. Here are a few tips:

- Write it in the third person.
- Start with your name. (Rebecca Waters is...)
- Keep it simple. People want to know a bit about you, but not your life story.
- Make it fun. Pique the interest of the reader. What makes you unique?
- Keep it in the present tense. The person you are now.
- Include your contact information. Not everything. You can say, for example, "You can follow Rebecca on Twitter @WatersAuthor."

You will write two professional bios. You need a short version and a longer version. Your one paragraph short bio will serve as the opening for your longer version. Think of the short version as your thesis statement and subsequent paragraphs as supporting evidence.

For example, in my initial short version I wrote:

"Rebecca Waters draws on her role as a wife, mother, and grandmother, as well as her vast experience as an educator and researcher for her writing. She and her husband, Tom, have been married for over forty years and have three grown daughters. Her daughters are all married and mothers themselves to five precious little ones."

At that time I hadn't published anything. I was starting my writing career. Check out what I crafted as my bio a few months later.

"Rebecca Waters draws on her role as a wife, mother, and grandmother, as well as her vast experience as an educator and researcher for her writing. Rebecca sees writing as both a gift and a ministry. Although she has published in professional journals in the field of education, Rebecca now turns her pen to fiction. She also enjoys freelance writing opportunities. Her articles may be found in *Chicken Soup for the Soul,* the *Home Health Aide Digest, Standard Publishing's Lookout Magazine, The Christian Communicator,* and *Church Libraries.* Rebecca's first novel, *Breathing on Her Own,* released on March 24, 2014 by Lighthouse Publishing of the Carolinas. It is available on Amazon in both print and Kindle versions."

Here is a later version:

"Rebecca Waters views writing as both a gift and a ministry. Her freelance writing includes works published in *Chicken Soup for the Soul,* the *Home Health Aide Digest, Standard Publishing's Lookout Magazine, The Christian Communicator,* and *Church Libraries.* Rebecca Waters' novel, *Breathing on Her Own* has been well received in the Christian fiction market. Rebecca shares her writing journey in her weekly blog, *A Novel Creation.* You can connect with her at www.WatersWords.com or follow her on Twitter @WatersAuthor."

Another version includes my credentials as a speaker and some of my educational background. I can tweak my bio to fit an audience or the theme of a conference.

You'll see a longer bio at the end of this book.

We'll talk about social media in the next chapter. You'll be making your bio for those accounts as well. Those bios are generally much shorter. Here is my Twitter bio as an example:

"Rebecca Waters @WatersAuthor. A Southern girl living in the Midwest with part of her heart still beating in Kosovo. Author. Jesus Follower."

Your Assignment: Write your bio in fewer than 100 words. Be sure to use third person.

Website

Now is the time to claim a website name and to begin building your website. I considered this job to be well out of my range of knowledge, skills and abilities. In the end, I prevailed on my oldest daughter to help me add buttons to my blog site and make it look like a website. It works. You can check it out at www.WatersWords.com. I've since discovered a number of free, user-friendly sites to help technologically challenged people like me.

The cost comes in buying a name for your site. I used GoDaddy to secure the name Waters Words, bringing us to the next point. Be strategic about selecting the name for your web address.

Although the title of my first novel, *Breathing on Her Own,* was available as a web name, I decided against it. I intended to publish more novels as well as nonfiction, so I wanted a site I could live with for a long time.

Before purchasing the name Waters Words, I made a list of possible names. The first four on my list were already taken. Having a list of possible site names handy made the process less stressful, and when my publisher asked for my web address to include in the front matter of the book, I was ready.

Before you publish you can post your bio, headshot, contact information, and blog on your website. Be sure to check in with your site regularly and update it frequently.

Social Media

You need social media. Social media is a valuable tool in building a platform. Building a platform takes time so we'll start with what you can do today.

Word of mouth remains the best marketing tool out there. Social media is a major part of today's word of mouth network. It is the number one way people are connecting with you and your work. You will need to set up a professional Facebook page as well as at least one other social media account. I use Facebook and Twitter. Two of my daughters use Instagram and Twitter as a main professional connection. I have an author friend who insists Facebook and Pinterest are essential for every writer.

> **The best accounts for you are the ones you feel most comfortable using.**

I suggest to new writers they start with Facebook and Twitter, even if they only use one of those at the beginning. My reason for setting up both accounts at same time is simply because it is best to set up the accounts with the same or similar names.

Your Facebook Business Page

Even if you haven't yet published, you'll want to look at this now because it's what I call low-hanging fruit. It is easy and readily available.

You may already have a personal Facebook page. That's where you post the news that your sister just had a baby or you attended a concert. Your personal page is great for connecting with people you already know. Your professional page is your opportunity for new people to connect with you as a writer.

People can "like" your page and receive notifications from you. You can post relevant content, graphics, links to your blog, schedules of your speaking engagements, pictures of you with your followers, your book cover or book trailer, links to radio interviews and so forth.

You can schedule your posts on your business page so they pop up when you are on vacation. You can create memes or load pictures to show up on the same date your book releases. I know some people who use their page as a host for their blog.

In addition, you can view analytics. You can see what posts work best for you, what posts are being shared, and how many views you are getting each week. Consistently engaging on your business page will ensure your information continues to show up in the newsfeed of your followers.

When you set up your page, be sure to use your professional headshot and choose a photo for your cover that reflects your brand. Once you publish, you can change the cover to show your book cover.

You can purchase ads through the page and you can pay to boost selected posts to go out to your entire Facebook list. I tend to go the freebie route when starting up.

Once you set up your account, pay attention to comments and posts made by your followers. Respond in a timely manner. This increases your visibility.

Initially, I set up my Facebook author page with the same name I had on my personal page. The marketing agent at my publishing house recommended I add "Author" to the mix so that my author page on Facebook is now "Rebecca Waters Author." To make sure I keep those accounts separate, I added my maiden name to my personal page.

The marketing agent then asked me about my other social media presence. I didn't have any. My youngest daughter came to the rescue and taught me a few Twitter basics. I opened a Twitter account as @WatersAuthor.

Part of the reason I like starting with these two platforms is because they work well together. I can write a message on my

Facebook page and have it automatically linked to my Twitter feed, allowing me to remain active on both sites with a single post.

Other Accounts

If you have a Pinterest account, you may want to explore the idea of using that account to connect with future readers. One author I know posts pictures of characters and settings in the Pinterest account. She keeps the account closed or secret until she's ready to engage readers. She uses the account first to plot and plan her novel and then a few months before the novel is released, she invites people to view the board.

I watched the same process unfold on Facebook when *New Life*, the movie was in production. Drew Waters, the director of the movie, placed pictures and quotes from the movie as well as tidbits from its production on Facebook. I can readily see how this would play out on Pinterest.

If you are writing a nonfiction book, you may find your audience through LinkedIn. Professionals in your field of expertise are more likely to use that account. It's a clear path to finding your perfect audience as well as keeping up with current trends in your field.

I know several authors who maintain an Instagram account. The point of social media for the author is to connect with readers. Use the social media platforms most used by your targeted audience. If you are comfortable with one facet of social media, use that to its full potential. Explore your options. Be creative.

A Word About Self-Promotion and Media Management

I've stated this before but it bears stating again. Eighty percent (80%) of your online presence should be about other people, writing in general, quotes, and notifications for the common good. Only twenty percent (20%) or less should be about you, your books, or your successes.

A writer friend recommended I use a media management system to plan, schedule, and send out messages to my social media accounts. I provided a series of entries about *Breathing on Her*

Own when it was released. I thought I was sending them to different groups. Unfortunately, every post I wrote went out to every group to which I belonged. Every day. Multiple times a day. I was inadvertently spamming my friends. I apologized. I learned how to remove some of the entries and took charge of the system to better manage my posts. Explore media management systems available to you. You can find free management systems such as Hootsuite or Buffer. These are valuable tools, but make sure you know how they work.

I also like Social Jukebox. This tool will tweet quotes they have in stock or other innocuous material you provide on a regular basis. With Social Jukebox, I maintain that 80/20 social presence. I may send a tweet out about my book being on sale and one about the beautiful sunshine. Social Jukebox sends one out on my behalf that is a quote from Ben Franklin and two more I've loaded into the system that tout the works of other writers.

Your Assignment: List the social platforms you already know and use. Then, find and list at least three new-to-you social media platforms.

Using Social Media to Build a Platform

Before we launch into building a platform, it's important to discuss CONSISTENCY. I have worked with authors who engage on social media sites occasionally or claim to host a blog, but only post on it once every few months…when they remember. I have also seen new authors who post only about themselves and their book. You want to use these tools to attract an audience, not drive them away.

> **In every area of building your platform and connecting with your audience, make consistency your mantra.**

Let's get started. What is a platform? A platform is often described as your tribe. It includes the people who follow you and share an interest in what you are doing. It may help to think of your platform as members of a target audience with whom you have connected.

Building a platform is essential to marketing yourself. Your audience needs a way to learn more about you and what you have to offer. There are several ways to establish that connection beyond tweeting.

In this section we'll look at blogging, creating a Facebook group, and building an email list. We'll talk a bit about Goodreads. Is there more? Yes. But if you are new to the writing game, these are the first steps you will want to pursue. Read each of these opportunities and decide what works for you.

> **You don't *need* to do it all. You *do need* to start somewhere.**

Writing a Blog

Blogging is your opportunity to produce content about who you are, what you believe, and what people can expect from you. Readers of your blog not only learn from the content you share, they come to hear your voice. Your message and way of connecting will resonate with some readers. Those readers will follow you. When you release a book or announce you are going to speak at a library in their area, those readers will support you. They will refer to you as a friend even if they've never met you.

I attended my first writing conference in Illinois. I loved the workshops and main sessions. The panel discussions were insightful and the opportunity to meet with agents and editors one-on-one was incredible. One of the greatest learning experiences turned out to be talking with other writers over lunch. All of the experienced writers I met maintained a blog. Consequently, I researched and mapped out a blog. I launched *A Novel Creation* six months later. It has appeared weekly since January 2013.

Most writers I talk with believe the biggest benefit of blogging is building a platform. While there is truth in that, the greater benefit is that blogging on a regular basis improves your writing. Through your posts you cultivate your voice and your brand.

However, the blog only works for you if you are consistent in delivering it. You don't need to write daily or even three times a week. Once a week is sufficient. Again, the key is consistency. I would argue that although at least once a week is ideal, I would be happier to see a writer or speaker post once a month than to post haphazardly or unpredictably.

Look at business websites. You will find blogs. Look at the websites of those in the publishing industry such as agents, publishing houses, and editors. You will find blogs. Even my church maintains a blog.

Read several blogs, research blogging, and examine web-based platforms available to host your blog. Some of those services are free. Others charge by the month. Most authors I meet use

Wordpress or Blogger. New hosts are always emerging. Find what works best for you.

Guest Posts

As you connect with other writers, speakers, and people in your industry, you will be asked to write guests posts on their blogs. Embrace those opportunities. Through these experiences you will likely increase your readership and expand your platform. As a writing exercise, draft a guest post. You may never use it, but then again someone may contact you requesting a post for the following week. I speak from experience. You'll have one ready, or at least close to ready. I keep a draft post about crafting a novel and one about a life experience that influences me as a writer on file. Reach out to other authors to post on your blog.

Interviews

I recommend writers create their own interview. Pose the questions you would love for others to ask you and answer them. I collect questions I see others being asked. I keep a list of questions I have been asked. When a blog host contacts me for a guest post but doesn't have a topic or direction for me, I offer an interview. I can pick and choose the questions and answers to fit the blog theme or word count determined by the host. I track what questions I use and where. I modify the questions or responses as needed. The beauty of doing this early on is that you'll never feel the pressure or time crunch to create a new post for someone else's blog. You can use some of these same questions to interview guests for your blog.

Analyzing Data from Your Blog

Take a serious look at analytics available for your blog on a regular basis. By regular, I mean once a quarter or every January and June. I'm not suggesting you become obsessed with the number of people reading or the number of comments left. Studying your blog performance will guide you in producing a better blog. For example, I learned I get the most readers, comments, and shares when my posts are between 600-1,000 words.

Building a Facebook Group

Another option to increase your platform is to create a Facebook group. My friend, Katharine Grubb mastered this type of platform building when she launched a group called 10 Minute Novelists. The group consists of writers from a variety of backgrounds writing in every genre imaginable. Members of the group are given guidelines or rules they must follow to remain in the group. It's a support group for writers. And it works. About a year after the group was formed, Katharine's book, *Write a Novel in Ten Minutes a Day,* was released. Katharine had an instant audience. She hadn't filled the page with self-promotion. Instead, she had actively participated in the group to support other writers. She built relationships. In doing so, Katharine built a platform.

You may want to build a Facebook group based on your genre. For example, if you write Civil War novels, you could organize a Facebook group interested in the topic. There you can share pictures, trivia, recipes, and stories. When you release your book, you will have a group of readers already interested in buying it.

Building an Email List and Newsletter

Occasionally, someone suggests email lists aren't all that important, saying there are better ways to communicate with your audience. I ask them if they've been to a sports event lately where someone was giving out t-shirts.

> "What did you have to do to get the shirt?" I ask.

> "Fill out a form."

> "Did they ask for your email address?"

They get the shirt that day, but later they receive an email. Email remains the number one contact information marketers seek.

Start with the contacts you already have. Store them in a database. Eventually you'll add contacts from book signings and speaking events. By the time *Breathing on Her Own* released, I had over 100 email addresses of people who wanted me to send them a message when the book went live on Amazon.

There are rules regarding sending out mass emails to people. You do not want to be known as a spammer. For that reason you'll want to use MailChimp or a similar email service to send info to your supporters.

Through the email service, you can send a monthly newsletter to your followers. The newsletter arrives via email. Two keys to making this work:

1. First make sure you load accurate emails into the service. Too many undeliverable addresses may result in you losing the service.
2. The second hint to making this work for you is to give something away in each newsletter. Viewers open the newsletter to see if they are among the winners that month. You want, actually need people to open the newsletter. The giveaways don't have to be grand. You can give away a $5 gift card or an e-book. It's a small price to pay to get the buzz about you and your book going.

Goodreads

Goodreads is a place where you need to have a presence. Not to market your books, though that can happen. The real value is in reading and engaging with others in discussions about books. It's a place to leave reviews, ask questions of authors, and find new books to read. Goodreads is more powerful than it appears on the surface. Try to check in on Goodreads at least once a week. You'll learn more about your target audience by engaging in conversations with them on Goodreads than any other platform. This is because unlike other social platforms, Goodreads discussions are all about books.

Three keys for maximizing your Goodreads experience:

1. Spend some time exploring the Goodreads site. Familiarity with the site will help you understand the set-up and many possibilities open to you. The browse button will lead you to Giveaways, New Releases, and more. Explore the community site and find groups you might like to join.
2. If you are a published author or are in the process of publishing a book, set up your Goodreads Author page. You have your bio and your headshot ready. You can post excerpts from your book or work in progress.
3. Browse books in your genre. These are books you want to read. When you are ready to draft your book proposal you'll have several books ready to list in the section "comparable titles."

> **To connect with others-**
>
> **To build a platform-**
>
> **Be consistent.**
>
> **Be consistent in communicating.**
>
> **Be consistent with your brand**

Your Assignment: Spend a half hour (minimum) exploring Goodreads. If you are already active on Goodreads, spend that time setting up a database of email addresses. You'll need them.

Looking Good on Paper

An essential part of your marketing includes creating business cards, bookmarks, and a compelling one-sheet. These are the pieces you can develop before you finish writing your book. All of these print pieces reflect your brand. They serve to connect you with people interested in what you write and what you have to say.

Business Cards

Your business card must have the following essential information: Your name, some sort of contact information, and at least one identifier.

Rebecca Waters

rebecca@waterswords.com

Author

That is basic. Essential information. You could print those on cardstock on your home computer. Is it ideal? No, but it actually has everything someone might need. I have received business cards that didn't have contact information or any sort of identifier. If I can't remember where I got the card, I file it in the circular file.

Let's go a bit beyond basic. I like a business card with a picture of the person on it. Remember that headshot we discussed earlier? I like putting a face with a name. I like having a picture as a reference when I try to locate that person on social media and discover there are at least twenty people by the same name.

You will note that in the example I put "Author" as my identifier. You may want to say "Author and Speaker" or "Writer: Freelance and Fiction." Whatever defines your role is what you want to include. A tagline or descriptor will enhance your branding. For example, my tagline might refer to Inspirational Fiction or Women's Fiction.

DO: For the contact information, you may put your email address instead of your website or you may want to include your Twitter handle.

DON'T: Do not put your personal address or personal phone number on the card. If you decide to share that information with someone in a face-to-face conversation, you can write it on your card.

DON'T: Do not give into the temptation to crowd your card with every possible contact. If you feel you must include your Twitter, Facebook, Instagram, Pinterest, LinkedIn, Snapchat, and every other account you ever signed up to do, list them alphabetically on the back of the card. If you have one you use more than the others, you can list it first and say, "You can also find me on…"

DO: Leave plenty of white space. I like white or light space where I can make a note to remind me specifics of meeting that person. I've also had opportunities to recommend books and websites in conversations. Having a space to write on a card serves both of us later in building relationships. I may email that person with, "We met over lunch at the XYZ writing conference. We were talking about your day job as a book promoter. I wondered if you'd be interested in being a guest on my blog?"

DON'T: Do not make your business card black. I know it's trendy and the white font seems to pop off the page, but receivers of the card can't make notes on it. And you can't easily change anything. One writer I know told me to ignore the web address because it had changed. Her card was midnight blue on both sides, making it impossible to write the new web address anywhere on the card. So if you insist on a dark color, make sure the other side is light.

DO: Keep it simple but true to your brand

DON'T: Do not use multiple fonts.

Bookmarks

I have read claims from several authors that people are more likely to keep a bookmark than a business card. Perhaps. Certainly if they use it, they will see you and your brand every time they open a book. I created bookmarks with the same information I have on my business card, but with an image of the book cover for *Breathing on Her Own*. I have given these away to people who read my book on an eReader because they still want an autograph. (I understand there is an app that allows you to autograph ebooks, but I'm not there yet.) One of the positive aspects of using a bookmark is that you have more space for needed information. You may want to use a bookmark even before you publish. Let people know what your book is about or who you are and when they can expect your work to be released.

One Sheet

The one-sheet or sell-sheet is usually constructed to sell your book to a publisher or agent. A one-sheet is, in essence, a visually appealing sell sheet for your book. Think of it as a full color ad for your book. It will have a compelling image relating to the story or character. It will have a blurb about your book and a tagline. The one-sheet will also feature your headshot, your bio, your contact information, and your writing credentials. If you have an agent, you will include that information as well.

Search the internet for templates and ideas to construct your one-sheet. Be thoughtful of the colors you use and be sure to capture the essence of you or your work using the least number of words possible. Seek endorsements Collect photos relative to you, your brand, or the subject of your book. Remember, this one-sheet should be a work in progress. Feel free to revise it when circumstances change or when you want to customize it to fit a particular group or situation. Starting the process now will save you time and headaches later. Once you have created the one-sheet, run it by your critique group or support team. They'll give you valuable input for future revisions.

Launching Your Book

You have finished drafting your book. You have probably revised it many times over and you're ready to take the next big step: Publishing. There are two main tracks for publishing. The first is to let someone else handle the details. This may be a traditional publishing house or a publisher you hire to do the job. The second is independently publishing your work. This is called "indie publishing," and more widely accepted than the early versions of self-publishing or "vanity publishing" routes.

Here are a few of the elements of marketing you need to explore at this stage. Employ the ones that you need when you need them. There is no specific order to these, with the exception of the book proposal. If you are pitching to an agent or acquisitions editor for a publishing house, you need to prepare your book proposal before you worry over any of the other elements.

Looking Good on Paper and in Front of a Publisher

The Book Proposal

Once you have penned a book, you need to create a book proposal to present your work to potential agents or publishers. Your proposal will look very much like a business plan for the book. Below is a skeleton of a book proposal. Some agents and publishers have a specific proposal format. It will likely include what you see here, but before you send anything off, check to see if they want or expect a specific order.

The working title of your book and your name appear in the header so that it appears on each page of the proposal. The title with your name below it will be centered next on the page. The body of your proposal will be set up as follows:

Premise: A sentence or two that captures the essence of the story.

Audience: Identify your intended audience. Who is likely to buy your book?

Comparable Titles: This is where you name the books most like yours. I have seen some authors list this as competition. I prefer comparable since there is room for all of us on the shelf. Look for books in your genre that target a similar audience.

Status: Where are you in the process? It can be *I have completed the project. I am in the revision stages for this complete work. The book is outlined and on schedule for completion by October 1...* You get the idea. A publisher wants to know you have a manuscript or have a reasonable timeline for completion. Note: If you are a new author it is best, though not necessary, to have a completed manuscript before approaching a publisher.

Size: This is where you note your word count. If you have not completed the work, give your projected word count.

Bio: Remember that bio you crafted? Copy and paste it into your proposal here.

Contact information: Be sure to include your email address as well as your snail mail address.

Synopsis. Specify your genre in the synopsis. Briefly describe the setting (no more than a paragraph), identify the crisis or problem to be solved, and describe the main characters. Share how the crisis is solved. If you have written a nonfiction work, list and describe each chapter.

A note here: I have had several new authors resist the notion of including the ending to their story in the synopsis. "I don't want to give it away," they tell me. YES, YOU DO! A startling reality for new authors is to learn that very few people at the publishing house actually read their book. A few read your synopsis. They may read the first fifty pages. They want to know you know how the conflict is resolved. They want to know it makes sense. They are not out to steal your idea, nor are they going to reveal your surprise ending and foil their own sales. They need to know you can deliver. Period.

The Elevator Pitch

The idea of the elevator pitch is being able to give your most compelling argument for why someone in the industry should be interested in hearing more from you in the thirty seconds to two minutes it would take to ride up an elevator.

Imagine yourself stepping onto an elevator with someone you immediately recognize as a prominent book agent for suspense novels. He pushes "floor three." You have a minute alone with him. What will you say to pique his interest in your unpublished novel about a crime-fighting farmer in Minnesota?

Let's look at what you do in those face-to-face meetings with people who can change the course of your career. We'll look at developing an elevator pitch and when and where to use it…since it's not likely to be on an actual elevator.

Start with a brief statement about who you are. Not your whole story. For the agent you can say, "Mr. So and So, I'm Joe Smith. I write suspense novels." In less than five seconds he knows you know him, he knows your name, and he knows what you write. You want to sound confident, so avoid apologizing or sounding unprepared, "I'm trying to write a suspense novel" or "One day I hope to be able to meet with you to talk about maybe getting my book published."

Your statement is your tagline. It is the same line you put in your bio and on your business card.

Your next statement will give your listener a glimpse at what you can deliver. "I have a completed manuscript where the unlikely hero is a Minnesota farmer who relies on his Navy SEAL training to rescue his niece from the clutches of someone with mysterious connections to a human trafficking ring." Remember that premise statement you crafted? That is your starting point.

The purpose of the elevator pitch is to pique the interest of the agent or publisher. Rehearse the pitch so it feels natural to you and could be delivered anywhere. You may find yourself pitching at a party where your host introduces you to her brother-in-law's fiancé, who happens to be a literary agent. It may take place on an airplane when you find yourself seated next to an acquisitions editor for a publishing house. Stranger things have happened, but in all likelihood, your elevator pitch will come into play when you have made an appointment with an agent or publisher at a writing conference. Follow these steps to prepare your pitch.

Step 1: Prepare a compelling elevator pitch for your manuscript.

Step 2: Practice the pitch until it feels natural and you can deliver it easily.

Step 3: Make an appointment with an agent or acquisitions editor of a publishing house.

Step 4: Ah, yes. There is a Step 4. Dress the part of a successful writer.

There is a rather old book out there called *Dress for Success*. I don't have a clue if it says anything about writers. What I do know is that while men seem to be able to pull off a more casual though clean look, women need to dress one step up from those already in the club.

Step 5: Write a note/email to the agent or editor, thanking him or her for the interview.

Flirting, Dating, and Getting Engaged (I actually have a talk on this one!)

If you choose to publish the book yourself, you need to research that path. A traditional publisher will hire a professional editor for you. Don't skip that step. A traditional publisher will provide a high resolution, professional book cover. Don't skip that step. And a traditional publisher will help you craft the blurb that goes on the back of your book.

I wrote a blog post called, "Flirting, Dating, and Getting Engaged." It describes marketing in terms of what people see when they pick up the book or scroll through a pile of books on Amazon. This is often your first contact with readers outside your mom and a circle of friends.

Flirting. The book cover and title catches the eye of the reader. Make sure the image on the front matches the content and the layout is such the title doesn't get "lost in the clouds" or something. Your publisher will run a few ideas by you, but it's okay to have researched your genre and sketched out a few ideas yourself. Go to a bookstore and study the covers of books in your genre. And as I said before, if you are indie publishing, make sure your cover is a high-resolution image. You can hire a graphic artist or use an online tool such as Canva to create your book cover.

Dating. If you were successful in the flirting stage, your potential reader has turned the book over, or in the case of Amazon, started reading the book blurb to see if they want to continue in this relationship.

Draft a compelling book blurb. If you have written a nonfiction work, tell how your book differs from other books. If you write fiction, give enough of the story to grab the reader's attention. Again, draw on the premise statement you used for your book proposal. Read the blurbs of popular authors in your genre. Learn through their example how much info you need to include.

Getting Engaged. A guy gives a girl a diamond ring. Your reader gives you a sale, and if you deliver what you promised, it could be a relationship that lasts forever.

You've Published, Now What?

Here we will look at a number of items needed to promote your book. The first is the media kit. We will also examine a book insert for the print version of your book, postcards, book trailers, visuals, giveaways, and one of the most important pieces -- getting reviews.

Media Kit

You have this. Seriously, if you have created the items you need to connect the face with the name and to look good on paper, you have most of the work done for you.

Though you can create an old-fashioned manila folder media kit, the likelihood of ever being asked for it is virtually nil. You will create a computer file you are able to send in total or in part to anyone, anywhere, anytime.

Include in your kit the following:

1. Your headshot
2. Your bio
3. Your book blurb from the back of your book
4. Interview questions asked and answered (I wouldn't send all of the questions. Pick and choose the ones relevant to your audience.)
5. Links to your website, your book, your blog
6. Endorsements or book reviews
7. Graphics or photos supporting your book
8. A press release. I have written several press releases for small "hometown" newspapers for my novels. I write them in third person and make the connection between the book and the hometown area and me. It works. Smaller papers like an article already written for them. They happily include the book title and where to buy it. I also write a press release for my university newsletter. They love to feature alumni finding success.

Place your media kit in a file on your website or at least have everything in a file on your computer.

Book Insert

After you write your stellar novel, consider drafting a book insert to accompany it. Any time you sell a book or give one away you can include this insert. You can produce this during that lull when your editor is beginning the process of polishing your book.

A book insert is a call to action.

When *Breathing on Her Own* released in 2014, my husband and I held a book launch party. In each book sold, we included a book insert. The next day, one woman contacted me to ask if she could purchase another book. She read the insert for my Christian fiction story. One call to action was to "donate a copy of the book to your church library." This woman wanted to do that. NOTE: Keep the call to action in the third person. "Leave a review for …at…." Not "*I* would appreciate a review…" or "Leave a review for *me*…"

Here is what I put on that first insert. It may give you a few ideas.

1. Invite your Facebook friends to read the book.
2. Have your book club or small group read the book.
3. Recommend/Review the book on Goodreads &/or Amazon.
4. Post the *Breathing on Her Own* Book trailer to your Facebook page or Pinterest page. You can find it on YouTube here: http://youtu.be/N6dVU7hO5rc
5. Invite the author to speak at your next club or church event, or writer's group meeting. The author is available in person or by Skype!
6. Tweet about the book #BreathingOnHerOwn
7. Tweet the author @WatersAuthor
8. Hit the "like" button on the author page. www.facebook.com/RebeccaWatersAuthor
9. Request a copy of the book at your local library.
10. Donate a copy of the book to your church library.
11. Give the book as a gift with a note inside from you.
12. Visit the author website at www.WatersWords.com

13. Review the book on Amazon
14. Most of all…enjoy the read

Breathing on Her Own is available on Amazon in print & on Kindle.

Ten actions on your insert is ideal. Make sure you have no more than fifteen. If I were doing this over, I would truncate number five, leaving off the part about "in person or by Skype" and eliminate numbers six, seven, and thirteen. I already asked them to review it on Amazon in number four. Writing is always about revising.

Postcards

I was a bit skeptical about the use of postcards. I shouldn't have been. A friend helped me design the postcards with my book cover on the front and the book blurb beside it. On the back, on the left side I included the Amazon link and my web address. I left room to write a message and mailed these to three area librarians. Two of them contacted me to speak for their book clubs. I mailed the remaining cards to book clubs and area church libraries. You can mail postcards inexpensively to bookstores, your college, high school, or other local groups.

Book Trailers

I have heard many seasoned authors and publishers say this is the best time to be a writer. Yes, the competition is fierce, but the media opportunities are endless. No longer do you need to hire a theatrical company to produce a video to promote you or your product. You can post your self-made interview or webinar on YouTube with virtually no production experience. Affordable programs and apps are available to produce professional looking book trailers.

Watch and study book trailers. Find a few trailers you like. They don't need to be in your genre. Study interesting, engaging trailers. Look for common elements. What made those trailers attractive? Was it the pacing? The music? Perhaps it was the simplicity of the message. Book trailers are visual. Writers tend to want to put too much text in the trailer. Avoid that pitfall. As you write your book, think about the images that move your story forward.

You can make a book trailer yourself using a program you purchase or a free app. The gal who put my first book trailer together used a program called Animoto Pro. It had a very professional look to it. If you use a free app, their logo stays on the trailer, but that was okay by me. The overall look was what I wanted.

If you're on a budget, there are other ways to create your trailer. You may want to use PowerPoint or another presentation format. I know one woman who used the built in camera and microphone on her computer to read a few lines from her book. Practice with that one. If you use your own equipment, I recommend you put a paper over the screen so you don't appear to be looking down all the time.

Visuals

What is the saying? A picture is worth a thousand words? You can create eye-catching memes, graphics, and infographics to capture your message and market your work. Memes and photos to sprinkle in your blogs, tweets, Instagram messages, and Facebook posts are no longer expensive for authors to make on their own.

You can use your camera to catch great photos as a backdrop for a quote from your book. There are a number of free images available to you as well. Be careful to not infringe on copyrighted pictures. I use Canva as a program to upload my own images and put them together with free templates.

Giveaways

New writers balk at the idea of giving away a copy of their book. Believe it or not, giveaways lead to sales. I've seen it happen. Giveaways spark a buzz about your book, look exactly like sales on your Amazon stats, boost your presence on Amazon, and lead to more reviews.

Giveaways take place in various settings. You can create a Goodreads giveaway, be part of a book event where you offer a giveaway, or give a book away to a lucky reader on a blog. It can be your blog or someone else's. I caution authors to limit where you are willing to mail a print version of your book. For example, I will offer a Kindle version of my book to anyone. I only offer a print version to people in the continental US. Out of the country shipping costs more than the book.

From time to time, your publisher may offer the e-book version of your book as a free book. This also promotes sales and reviews.

Reviews

You want reviews. Honest reviews. Reviews are a powerful marketing tool. You will use phrases from reviews in your tweets and other social media messages. You will take excerpts from good reviews for your one-sheet and media kit.

How do you get reviews? I ask. I don't ask for good reviews. I ask for honest reviews. If I give a book away, I say, "And I hope you'll be so kind as to leave an honest review. If you don't like the book, that's okay. Just be specific about what you didn't like."

I ask friends. I ask followers of my blog. I post my goal for fifty book reviews by a certain date on my Facebook author page. Ask.

Another way to get reviews is to ask book reviewers who host blogs or review for websites. Search for people who review books in your genre. Email a request to them. Reviewers often offer guidelines for the request. Usually, they ask for a free digital copy of your book to review. DO NOT PAY for a book review. That is wrong on so many levels.

By the time I launched my first novel, *Breathing on Her Own*, I had collected at least 100 emails from people asking me to let them know when the book was published. I did. I sent individual emails to them telling them the book had been released. I asked them to consider being part of my team. All I asked them to do was to download the book, read it, and give an honest review. I told them they didn't even have to like it. From everything I've read,

Amazon takes you seriously as an author if you have 100 reviews. Having Amazon take you seriously has to be helpful in the marketing efforts, right?

I told them if they wrote a review, good or bad, I would be grateful. I promised that as soon as I had 100 reviews, no matter where they came from, I was putting names in a hat from my team and giving away prizes. Having 100 reviews is worth celebrating.

Once a person agreed, I sent a big thank you. I sent a "how to write a review" sheet so they knew where to go and how to post it on Amazon. I emailed team members to tell them how many reviews I had on a regular basis. Over thirty members of the group posted a review in the first five months. Most were pretty good, too. The 100th review came around nine months after the book launched. I was true to my word. Everyone who had agreed to be part of my team was in the drawing even if they hadn't written a review. I drew names and sent prizes. I sent gift cards to Starbucks, Amazon gift cards, journals, e-books, and elaborate handmade bookmarks.

I also posted how to write a review on my blog. I discovered people want to review your book. One reason they don't do it is because they don't know how. Sometimes they don't see how their voice matters. But it does. The more reviews you get, the more exposure your book gets on Amazon and other venues. I was talking with a stranger in line at the license bureau. The conversation came around to the fact I'm an author. It turned out she's a reader. Good match. She asked me the name of my book and as I said it, she typed it into her Goodreads account. "Hey, 4.7 stars! That's great." She ordered it then and there.

One other way to get reviews is by sending copies of your book to book reviewers. You can also search the term "book reviews" and find lists of readers who will review your book. You send them a book and they write a review. Some of these reviewers post on their blog, others review for Goodreads and/or Amazon. Amazon ranks reviewers, so grabbing that list is a good way to find strong reviewers.

Your Assignment:

Okay, I've loaded you down with a ton of ideas and your head is swirling. Jot down a short list of your favorites. Sketch a business card or a bookmark. Create scene cards for a book trailer. Do whatever you like here. It's your choice. It's your opportunity to freely explore any and all possibilities. Putting them in this book preserves them for that time when you are ready to use those ideas.

The Book Launch and Other Events

Book Launch

A book launch is an event designed to celebrate the birth of a new book. The purpose is to generate buzz about the book and boost sales.

There are at least two types of book launches. The first is a traditional face-to-face gathering of people and the second is a virtual book launch. Most people think they should have the book launch the minute the book is released. You'll fare better if you hold the launch three or four weeks after the book is released. And since my book took place in both Florida and Ohio, I held two launches.

The Traditional Book Launch

I wanted a traditional launch for my first novel. I wanted to celebrate with friends and family. My husband and I had lived in the area for a very short time, so I invited neighbors I didn't know and people from our church. However, we grew up in that area so I invited friends from high school and family as well. What a fun reunion.

During the outdoor event by the lake, we had a flat screen television hooked up with the book trailer looping, a table where people could sign in and enter their name in a drawing, a beautiful spread of finger foods, outdoor tented canopies and lawn chairs. I greeted everyone and at one point addressed everyone. I thanked them for coming, thanked those who helped pull the event together, read the dedication to my mother and introduced her, and thanked my precious husband for all of his support. A couple of family members and friends kept the food trays filled and my sister-in-law manned the book table. I mingled.

How does having thirty to forty people celebrate the beginning of a book help market it? For one thing, those people talked about it. A lot. Following the event, I had several people who weren't present at the event asking me about the book.

One woman purchased a book for herself on launch day and returned after reading the insert to purchase a second one for her church. After the event, another woman submitted the book to her book club. They read my book next in their rotation and left reviews. I met a new neighbor a few weeks later who recognized my name and said, "You're the one who wrote that book, aren't you?" People talk. I am a people person. For me, a face-to-face launch made sense.

Another reason I wanted a launch is that I wanted pictures. I wanted evidence the book was real and people really knew about it. That may sound silly, but to me it was a credibility piece. The photos turned out to be great for Facebook, Twitter, and my blog.

The Virtual Book Launch

A growing trend is to offer a virtual book launch on Facebook or another platform. Go to your author Facebook page and create an event. Invite friends to your event. Tell them they can invite their friends as well.

Before your launch, plan what you will say and do. What will you share? People want to know where you got the idea for your book. They like to hear or read BRIEF excerpts. Type your posts in a Word document so you can simply cut and paste to keep the pace of your event going. I suggest placing pictures you want to include such as your book cover and memes on your desktop so you don't have to search your files during the event. And you can actually "pin" the pictures ahead of time to schedule when they pop up.

Be sure to thank everyone for coming. Have them sign in as they arrive. You can play games and offer giveaways. One of my author friends held an online scavenger hunt. I recommend you employ the assistance of a friend who will monitor posts, make sure everyone is in the drawing and take care of the logistics. That person doesn't need to be with you. He or she can chat with you via personal messaging on Facebook so you can focus on keeping the party going.

You can give away an e-book version of your book, gift cards, or other artifacts connected to your book. Set a specific time frame and stick to it.

Personal Appearance Events

By events, I'm talking about book signings, speaking engagements, book club meetings, and so forth. It may sound old school to some, but I like interacting with other people. I'm convinced that people I personally meet will be some of my best word-of-mouth advertisers. My evidence? The first four events following the publication of *Breathing on Her Own* were organized by people who knew me, read my book, and were excited to help. They set up those events for me. Events garner book purchases and reviews, and more importantly, create a buzz about the book.

How can you get the most out of the event? I ask people to sign-in at these events, giving me their name and email address. I send them a thank you for attending. I ask them to "like" my author Facebook page. I offer them guidelines on how to write a review.

Your Assignment:

Research book launches. List at least three ideas you find that you will be able to use when your book is ready.

Develop a Marketing Plan

Developing a marketing plan is important. In fact, your publisher may ask you for your plan. My publisher said it takes nine months to a year for a book to grow legs. I mapped my plan for twelve months and revised it along the way.

A marketing plan, like your business plan, needs to have specific goals. Set a time frame to meet each. You will always have a "next step" and stay on target to market your book. For example, one goal for this *Writing to Publish* is to garner thirty reviews by the end of the release year and 100 reviews within three years. (Hint: You can be one of them!)

Start with a calendar. Your marketing begins in the months before your book is released. Use social media and your blog to begin to build interest. Let your followers know when the book is scheduled for release and collect email addresses of those interested. Set up an events calendar to include your launch and book signings.

Determine your budget. You can find ways to do most things affordably, but if you want your book trailer to have a quality look, you may want to invest money there since this will be something you use over and over. On the other hand, you may decide to work with other authors you know to create a blog tour rather than paying someone else to do that for you. Your budget will determine if you rent a venue for your book launch or do as I did and have it in your back yard or church.

One literary agent and advocate for writers uses a baseball analogy in talking about marketing. In baseball, batting .300 is a good percentage. It means a good baseball player may strike out or get out approximately two of three times at bat. A return of thirty percent of my effort is good. I can live with that. It simply means not everything I try will work. I can't put all my heart into one strategy, hoping my ad/quote/news release or whatever will go viral and make everyone in the country buy my book. I may try ten different things. If three of them work, I'm batting .300…as good as a big league hitter.

Marketing is a process. You only have so much time and energy. But you don't have to do everything by yourself. Consider enlisting the assistance of others to do those things you feel ill-equipped addressing.

> **Make marketing part of your writing habit.**

This isn't the end of the journey. You will continue to find new ways to connect with agents, publishers, and readers. This book will get you started and on your way to a successful career in writing.

Resources

Prompts

As promised, here are a few prompts to get you started:

What is your favorite holiday and why?

Do you have a favorite Thanksgiving memory?

Describe each of the four seasons where you live.

If asked, what song would you choose as your theme song? Why?

What is your earliest childhood memory?

Who was your favorite teacher and why?

How has technology impacted your life?

Describe the five things in your life that bring you the most joy.

What are your ten favorite movies?

If you could choose a movie star to portray you in the story of your life, who would you choose? Why?

Those are a few choices. You can also checkout *Writer's Digest* at http://www.writersdigest.com for a weekly prompt.

Template for Writing a Query Letter

      A query letter is just that –a letter. It is a formal letter to an editor, asking if he or she is interested in publishing a story or article you will write. There is a strategy, though. Here is an example of how to write a query for a magazine article. A book query you would send to an agent will contain more information about the plot, genre, and so forth.

Your name

Return address

email address

phone number

Date

Address of publication to which you're submitting

Greeting/Salutation

1st paragraph- This is your hook. State the premise of the article. You will likely use this as the opening line of your article. It shows the problem you will address.

2nd paragraph- Describe how your article will address the problem identified.

Ex. This 1,200 word article will examine three strategies parents can employ to teach children time management (then you name those three strategies).

3rd paragraph- Offer your credentials to write the article.

4th paragraph- This will be your "sign off" paragraph. [Thank you for considering this article. I understand it would be on speculation only. I look forward to hearing from you.]

Sincerely,

Your name

NOTE: This is important. If you are submitting a query via email, be sure to put your name and the topic or title of the article, <u>in the subject line of your email</u>. If you need to contact the editor in the future, your query will be easily located.

Gearing Up Checklist (Marketing Yourself and Your Writing)

- ✓ Professional headshot
- ✓ Bio short version
- ✓ Bio long version
- ✓ Secure website name
- ✓ Set up Facebook author page
- ✓ Set up Twitter account
- ✓ Explore or set up other social media account (optional)
- ✓ Acquire a free social media management system, such as Hootsuite
- ✓ Draft a 600-word guest post
- ✓ Collect and answer interview questions
- ✓ Begin organizing an email list
- ✓ Create a monthly newsletter
- ✓ Enroll in MailChimp or another email service for mass mailings
- ✓ Explore Goodreads and engage in a group
- ✓ Design a business card
- ✓ Begin collecting elements for your one-sheet

Publishing Checklist

- ✓ Create a book proposal
- ✓ Prepare and practice your elevator pitch
- ✓ Choose a publishing path and research what is required of you
- ✓ Design an eye-catching book cover
- ✓ Write a compelling book blurb
- ✓ Create a media kit

- ✓ Draft a book insert
- ✓ Make postcards with your book image on them
- ✓ Make or contract someone to make a book trailer for your book
- ✓ Put together a set of memes and graphics
- ✓ Explore giveaway options
- ✓ Plan a book launch
- ✓ Write out a marketing plan that is specific and time-bound
- ✓ Finally, enjoy the satisfaction of becoming a published author!

Other Resources

Bell, James Scott. The Art of War for Writers: Fiction Writing Strategies, Tactics, and Exercises. Cincinnati: Writer's Digest Books, 2009.

Writer's Market. Cincinnati: Writer's Digest Books

Kawasaki, Guy and Shawn Welsh. A.P.E.: Authors, Publishers, and Entrepreneurs- How to Publish a Book. N.p: Nononina, 2012.

Writer's Digest This writer's journal is available in a print copy delivered to your door. You can access articles, writing prompts, and news about the publishing community on their website: http://www.writersdigest.com

ABOUT THE AUTHOR

Rebecca Waters' writing and publishing adventure began in second grade. Her teacher submitted her short story to the school newspaper. She loved writing, but the opportunity to be just like her teacher was an even bigger draw. After completing her B.A. degree in Education at the University of South Florida, Rebecca taught for eighteen years in the public schools where she coached the Young Authors program. A lifelong learner, Rebecca completed her master's degree at the University of Cincinnati. Her thesis, "How Dialogue Journals Foster Growth in Reading and Writing" became the springboard for further research in writing. This led her to a doctoral degree, also from the University of Cincinnati. Her dissertation examined the revision activity of writers in the early childhood classroom. Rebecca taught for the next fourteen years in the teacher education program at Cincinnati Christian University. Writing during this period of her life centered on educational research. Retiring early, Rebecca turned her pen to crafting fiction. Her first two novels, *Breathing on Her Own* and *Libby's Cuppa Joe* have fared well in the contemporary Christian fiction market. Forever the teacher, Rebecca has presented at numerous conferences and writing workshops. She is active in the Ohio Chapter of American Christian Fiction Writers where she has the opportunity to coach and encourage new writers. The topics covered in *Writing to Publish* began with her research in the field of writing. Much of the text has been honed through speaking engagements, blog posts, and articles she published in periodicals such as *Language Arts, The Christian Communicator,* and *Church Libraries.* Rebecca has also published a novella, *Courtesy Turn,* in the Anthology, *From the Lake to the River*. Her work may be found in several *Chicken Soup for the Soul* books. For speaking engagements or questions, send an email inquiry to rebecca@waterswords.com. You can also follow Rebecca on Twitter (@WatersAuthor) or on Facebook (Rebecca Waters Author). You will find her weekly blog at www.WatersWords.com.

www.ingramcontent.com/pod-product-compliance
Lightning Source LLC
Chambersburg PA
CBHW071408290426
44108CB00014B/1727